EASY SPANISH COOKBOOK

Easy

SPANISH
COOKBOOK

Recipes to Bring Home
the Flavors of Spain

NOREMA SALINAS

**ROCKRIDGE
PRESS**

To my husband, Luis, thank you for your humorous support and knowledge of your Spanish culture. To my three precious jewels: Regi, Edu, and Adri. Now you have a cookbook of our favorite Spanish family recipes!

For general information on our other products and services or to obtain technical support, please contact our Customer Care Department within the United States at (866) 744-2665, or outside the United States at (510) 253-0500.

Rockridge Press publishes its books in a variety of electronic and print formats. Some content that appears in print may not be available in electronic books, and vice versa.

TRADEMARKS: Rockridge Press and the Rockridge Press logo are trademarks or registered trademarks of Callisto Media Inc. and/or its affiliates, in the United States and other countries, and may not be used without written permission. All other trademarks are the property of their respective owners. Rockridge Press is not associated with any product or vendor mentioned in this book.

Interior and Cover Designer: Mando Daniel
Art Producer: Janice Ackerman
Editors: Britt Bogan & Justin Hartung
Production Manager: Riley Hoffman
Production Editor: Melissa Edeburn
Photography: © 2020 Darren Muir. Food styled by Yolanda Muir.
ISBN: Print 978-1-64611-786-4 | eBook 978-1-64611-787-1
R0

Contents

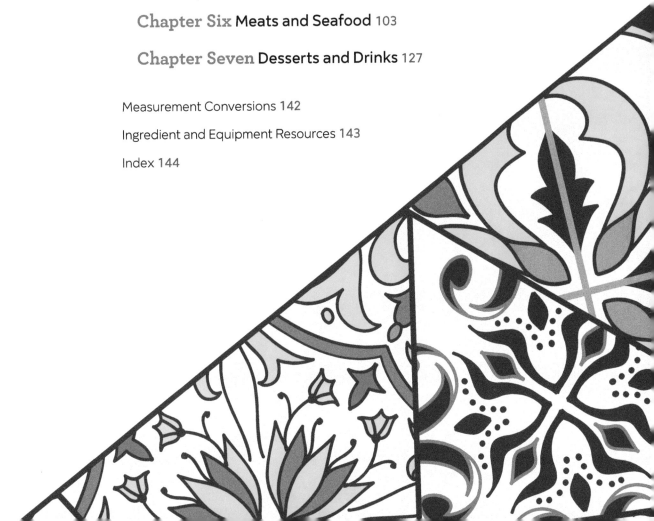

Introduction

Diversity is the spice of life, and it's also what triggered my passion for food. Raised in the cosmopolitan San Francisco Bay Area by a Brazilian mother and Bolivian father, I had many opportunities to travel and experience the world's cuisines. My love of Spanish food started when I moved to Spain as a teenager with my family. I vividly remember my first lunch at my new school and how utterly surprised I was by the delicious three-course meal that was served. It was then that I realized the importance of food in this wonderful country.

When I returned to Spain after college, my passion for Spanish food was revived with weekend trips to the medieval city of Segovia for suckling lamb, to the Basque Country for *pintxos* (small one- or two-bite dishes), to Asturias for saffron white bean–clam stew, and to Galicia for barnacles and spider crab. It was during this time that I truly understood that all gatherings and outings in Spain revolve around good food, good drink, and vivacious company.

In 1991, I hosted a dinner party at my home in Madrid, and Spanish fashion designer Modesto Lomba was one of my guests. He was so impressed with the meal, he convinced me to start Norema Salinas Catering, my pioneering modern catering business in Madrid. My clients included Gucci, Chanel, and BMW, and I had the honor of serving notable people such as the king of Spain, Prince Albert of Monaco, Pedro Almodóvar, David Beckham, Gwyneth Paltrow, and Paz Vega. Through my business, I learned to appreciate the classic dishes of Spain, as well as the cutting-edge creations that have made the country so prominent on the culinary map.

Some of my favorite memories are of afternoons spent feeding my family gazpacho (pages 62 and 64) and paella (page 82) or Vine Shoot–Grilled Lamb Chops (page 115) and Baker's Potatoes (page 52). We would linger at the table, having great conversations after dessert and coffee, enjoying the sunshine.

Now living in the Oakland Hills, we have managed to re-create our favorite Spanish food. The day after Thanksgiving, we cook a huge *cocido madrileño* (Madrid-style chickpea stew) for friends. Brunches at home consist of paella, *tortilla española* (Spanish potato and onion frittata), gazpacho, and sangria.

Since moving to the Bay Area with my Spanish family, I have learned not only how to reproduce traditional Spanish cuisine with local products but also how to adjust my recipes to suit the fast-paced American lifestyle. It is my pleasure to share my knowledge with you so you can make the healthy and delectable cuisine of Spain in your home.

Viva España!

CHAPTER ONE

Spanish Food 101

You can bring Spain's classic dishes to your table quickly and easily with the tips and tricks in this chapter. You'll discover the ingredients and cooking equipment you'll need to make authentic Spanish cuisine, as well as substitutions for ingredients and equipment not readily available outside of Spain. Nearly all of the recipes in this book can be made with an hour or less of active cooking time. Certain dishes, such as paella, may be slightly more time-intensive, but they're certainly worth the extra effort. Here's to introducing the flavors of Spain to your family and friends at home!

Spanish Cooking Staples

The staples and equipment you'd find in a typical Spanish household are common to most modern-day kitchens, and you may already have almost everything you need to create the recipes in this book. There are a few ingredients you won't be able to find at your local market, but I will tell you where you can source them online and even identify great substitute ingredients, should you prefer not to order them. Certain staples and equipment, such as a paella pan and a clay *cazuela* (casserole dish), can enhance the authenticity and presentation of the recipes. Others, like a garlic press, can help expedite your prep work. I'll describe these items later on as either Must-Haves or Nice-to-Haves.

INGREDIENTS

These are staples you will need to cook almost every recipe in this book.

MUST-HAVES
The following ingredients are integral to traditional Spanish recipes and can be found in any major grocery store.

Extra-virgin olive oil: Olive oil is a key component of the well-known Mediterranean diet (a style of healthy eating that emphasizes whole grains, lots of vegetables, fruit, nuts, seafood, and modest amounts of meat) and is ever-present in Spanish cuisine. It is a prominent ingredient in dressings, sauces (such as *mojo*), and gazpacho, as well as for cooking and frying. For deep-frying, choose a light, refined olive oil instead of an extra-virgin variety.

Garlic: Fresh garlic flavors rice, noodles, fish, and beef dishes, as well as stews, soups, and sauces. It also takes the starring role in dishes such as White Garlic Gazpacho (page 62), a dish also known as *ajoblanco* (meaning "white garlic").

Red pepper flakes: The spicy kick of pepper flakes is perfect for certain fish dishes sautéed with garlic and as the finishing touch for tapas.

Saffron: Known as "red gold," saffron is synonymous with Spanish cuisine. It is used for its lovely flavor, aroma, and color in stews and noodle and rice dishes. Although it is expensive, only a few strands are needed for any recipe.

Sea salt: Sea salt is indispensable in Spanish cuisine. Fine-textured sea salt is a staple for general cooking, and flaky Maldon or Ibiza salt is ideal to finish off meat dishes, tapas, and mushrooms.

Short-grain rice: Short-grain rice is a go-to in Spain because it releases starch that produces a moist and sticky texture. Although Spanish short-grain bomba rice (see page 3) is not widely available at major grocery stores, Arborio or Carnaroli rices are good substitutes.

Smoked paprika: The smoky aroma, unique flavor, and color of paprika make it a favorite for stews and rice dishes.

Tomatoes: Tomatoes are a Spanish favorite and feature prominently in the country's cuisine. Canned tomatoes can be used in stews and in rice and noodle recipes in place of fresh.

NICE-TO-HAVES

For a truly authentic flavor experience, these ingredients are nice additions to your collection of Spanish staples.

Anchoas españoles (Spanish anchovies): Premium anchovies in Spain are from Cantabria in northern Spain or from l'Escala in Catalonia. It is important to use the best-quality olive oil–packed anchovies you can find. You can source anchovies from both regions online.

Bomba rice: This short-grain rice is widely used for rice dishes and stews in Spain. There are several brands available online.

Bonito del norte: This albacore tuna is caught off the Bay of Biscay in the North Atlantic. While any canned albacore tuna can be substituted, premium canned bonito del norte can be found online.

Chorizo: The smoky flavor of this hard-cured sausage, which can be sweet or spicy, makes it a favorite for Spanish stews. Spanish chorizo is available online. My favorite brand is Palacios.

Cuttlefish ink or squid ink: Squid ink is essential for several representative and traditional dishes and, unfortunately, it has no substitute. Your local fishmonger or an upscale market may carry it, or you can source it online. Buy it in small individual packets, since most recipes won't require much. I like to use El Sison because it comes in four 4-gram packets.

Pimentón de la Vera (smoked paprika): While any smoked paprika will suffice for my recipes, pimentón de la Vera is the most authentic. This subtle, smoky-flavored paprika can be easily sourced online. If you like spice, I recommend you purchase picante (spicy) pimentón.

Piparras peppers: These vinegary, fiery semisweet Basque peppers are traditionally enjoyed with legume dishes, potato salad, and *pintxos* served in the Basque Country, such as *Gildas de mejillón* (Mussel, Pepper, and Olive Skewers, page 24). Order them online.

Spanish Wines

In Spain, a meal without wine is like a garden without flowers. Love of wine is embedded in Spanish culture. Eating, drinking wine, and socializing go hand in hand. Spanish wines are widely available in the United States. Here are the top 10 Spanish wine varietals:

Tempranillo (red)

Tasting notes: cherry, plum, figs, cedar, tobacco, pepper

Regions: Rioja, Castilla y Léon, Extremadura

Pairing: game, meat, stews, poultry, and charcuterie; Manchego and Idiazabal sheep's milk cheeses

Garnacha (red)

Tasting notes: anise, tobacco, berries, black tea

Regions: Catalonia, Navarra, Castilla–La Mancha, Madrid

Pairing: beef, lamb, and fish; Emmental, Jack, Camembert, and Gruyère cheeses

Monastrell (red)

Tasting notes: blackberry, chocolate, smoke, pepper

Regions: the Levante, Balearic Islands, Castilla–La Mancha

Pairing: meat, lamb, rabbit, stews, rice, and mushrooms; mild and smoked Cheddar, Manchego, Parmesan, pecorino, and smoked Gouda cheeses

Mencia (red)

Tasting notes: pomegranate, licorice, red fruit, floral

Region: Castilla y Léon

Pairing: game, lamb, meat, rabbit, cured ham, sausage, rice dishes with meat

Bobal (red)

Tasting notes: berries, dried green herbs, violets, cocoa

Regions: Castilla–La Mancha, the Levante

Pairing: chicken, rabbit, octopus, rice dishes with fish, seafood, legume stews, and grilled foods

Verdejo (white)

Tasting notes: herbaceous, lime, grapefruit, vanilla, wood

Region: Castilla y Léon

Pairing: white fish, shellfish, garlic

Godello (white)

Tasting notes: apple, floral, mineral, herbaceous

Region: Galicia

Pairing: white fish and shellfish

Albariño (white)

Tasting notes: stone fruit, jasmine, freshly cut grass

Region: Galicia

Pairing: fried tapas, charcuterie, fish, and shellfish; burrata, Gouda, Manchego, and goat cheeses

Viura (white)

Tasting notes: tropical fruit, apple, citrus

Regions: Rioja, Catalonia

Pairing: charcuterie, white meat, fish, shellfish, pasta, and rice; Cheddar, Fontina, Manchego, Jack, triple crème, Camembert, and Brie cheeses

Palomino (sherry)

Tasting notes: dry, saline, high acid

Region: Andalucía

Fino sherry: Fermented under a blanket of yeast and made with high-acid grapes grown in chalky white soils, this is the driest, most saline style of sherry.

Pairing: raw seafood

Manzanilla sherry: A slightly more delicate coastal version of fino aged in the cellars of the town Sanlúcar de Barrameda. It has a salty tang.

Pairing: salty snacks, peanuts, potato chips, olives, fried seafood

EQUIPMENT

Almost every recipe in this book can be made with the following equipment.

MUST-HAVES

These are all common kitchen tools that you likely already have.

Blender: A blender is necessary to make gazpacho and various sauces.

Cast-iron skillet: A large cast-iron skillet (at least 12 inches) is used to make paella and *fideuà* (noodles) and to sear lamb chops, pork, and beef loins.

Cutting boards: Cutting boards are necessary for your kitchen prep tasks such as cutting up the onions, garlic, and peppers to make a *sofrito*. To avoid cross-contamination, it is important to use separate labeled boards for fruit and vegetables, meat and poultry, and dry ingredients such as bread.

Mortar and pestle: A mortar and pestle is important for grinding spices and herbs. It can be wood, metal, or ceramic.

Sauté pans, skillets, saucepans, and soup pots: Various sizes of these pans and pots are used for everything from frittatas to rice and noodle dishes to stews.

Sieves: Sieves in different sizes are necessary to strain gazpacho and sauces to ensure a creamy texture.

Skimmer: A skimmer, which is a flat metal spoon with holes, is used to lift food out of oil when deep-frying. It's also useful for serving paella and rice dishes.

Stick blender: A stick blender, or immersion blender, is used to make mayonnaise and aioli, as well as other sauces.

These items will facilitate your food prep and/or add to a more authentic Spanish presentation.

Box grater (stainless steel): Many Spanish recipes call for grated tomato. Using a box grater will facilitate this task and expedite making dishes such as *pan amb tomàquet* (Tomato Toast, page 16).

Garlic press: Most Spanish recipes call for minced garlic, and a garlic press can do this quickly.

Hinged frittata pan (10-inch): With this pan, you can effortlessly flip your Spanish *tortilla* to perfection. They are easy to find online.

Mandoline: A mandoline can quickly slice potatoes and onions thinly for *tortilla española* (Spanish Potato and Onion Frittata, page 36), as well as cut onions for stews and rice and noodle dishes.

Paella pan: While a cast-iron skillet will suffice, paella is ideally made in a paella pan. Small to large paella pans are widely available online and in specialty cookware stores.

Terra cotta cazuela: A typical round terra cotta Spanish *cazuela* (casserole dish) makes for a more authentic presentation. They are easy to find online.

The Spanish Dining Experience

Spaniards generally eat more often than Americans, with smaller meals spread out throughout the day: breakfast (*desayuno*), midmorning snack (*almuerzo*), lunch (*comida*), afternoon snack (*merienda*), and dinner (*cena*). Breakfast is similar to a continental breakfast, eaten between 6:00 a.m. and 9:00 a.m., and can consist of coffee, orange juice, yogurt, toast (topped with olive oil, grated tomato, and sea salt or butter and jam), churros, or pastries. Between 11:00 a.m. and noon, Spaniards have a midmorning snack, such as a sandwich (*bocadillo*) or a tapa with a beer, coffee, or chocolate milk. Lunch, the most important meal of the day, is eaten between 1:30 p.m. and 3:30 p.m. Though traditionally colleagues, family, or classmates would share a three-course meal over the span of two hours, these days lunch is often limited to just an hour. The afternoon snack, served between 5:00 p.m. and 6:30 p.m., coincides with the end of the school day and in some cases the end of the workday. Kids have milk, a sandwich, and a pastry or cookies. Adults will have another tapa, sandwich, and a cup of coffee or tea. Dinner, eaten between 9:00 p.m. and 10:30 p.m., is when families gather for a one-course meal and share the details of their day, then retire to the living room before going to bed.

CULINARY REGIONS OF SPAIN

Each of the many regions of Spain is a culinary treasure, with unique dishes that are an integral part of the local heritage. The Cantabrian, Celtic, and Mediterranean Seas around Spain and the country's various mountain ranges, valleys, and rivers make regional Spanish cuisine truly diverse.

Andalucía

Andalucía, Spain's southernmost region, has a rich food culture that forms part of the renowned Mediterranean diet—fish, fruit, vegetables, and olive oil. Beach cafés serve delicacies such as skewers of sardines, wedge clams, white shrimp, and fried smelt. One of Andalucía's most famous dishes is *lubina a la sal* (Salt-Roasted Sea Bass, page 118).

Aragón, Navarra, and Rioja

These three regions in northern Spain are known for their stews and grilled meats. Navarra, the garden of the Basque Country, is famous for its *menestra de verduras* (Vegetable Mélange, page 48). Rioja wine pairs exquisitely with the area's succulent bean and pork stews and lamb dishes. In fact, the grape vines are often used for grilling *chuletillas de cordero al sarmiento* (Vine Shoot–Grilled Lamb Chops, page 115).

Asturias and Cantabria

The cuisine of Asturias and Cantabria is based on a wealth of seafood from the Cantabrian Sea and cattle, game, cheese, and legumes from the region's mountains and valleys. The region is known for dishes such as *fabada* (white bean and pork stew)—a wonderful treat after a hike up to the mountain village of Tresviso—and *flan de queso* (Cheese Flan, page 134) from a delightful road-side restaurant in the town of Cahecho.

Basque Country

A big part of the food culture in the Basque Country dates to 1870, when *txokos* (gastronomical societies) started in San Sebastián, gathering to socialize, cook, eat, and drink. Today, the region boasts 33 Michelin stars and is known for its creative *pintxos*, artisanal bites, and *sidrerias* (cider houses), where salt cod omelets and grilled steak are washed down with hard cider.

Castilla–La Mancha

Castilla–La Mancha is home to the windmills made famous in *Don Quixote*. The region's Manchego cheese is its best ambassador. The pastoral cuisine of the region features dishes such as *migas de pastor* (toasted day-old bread with pork and grapes), *pisto manchego* (Spanish Ratatouille, page 58), and *sopa de ajo* (garlic soup).

Castilla y León

Castilla y León's cuisine features products of the earth made into hearty dishes to combat the region's extreme weather. It is famous for its roasted lamb, goat, and pork made in wood-fired clay ovens. Delicious hearty stews like *cocido maragato* (chickpea-pork stew) are perfect to warm and energize you for the Astorga stage of the Camino de Santiago (pilgrimage to Santiago).

Catalonia

Bordering France, Catalonia has the most refined cuisine in Spain. It is home to the vibrant city of Barcelona and is the cradle to Ferran Adriá, the pioneer of the molecular gastronomy movement. His restaurant, El Bulli, was named best restaurant in the world for many years.

Extremadura

Extremadura is home to the jewel of Spanish cuisine, *jamón ibérico de bellota*, ham produced from acorn-fed black Iberian pigs. In addition to *jamón*, the region's rural cuisine is represented best by chorizo (sausage seasoned with Spanish paprika), *torta del casar* (creamy sheep's milk cheese), and cherries from the Jerte Valley.

Galicia

Galicia is known for the best seafood in Spain, which comes from the sea, estuaries, and rivers of the region. Octopus, stone crab, oysters, clams, and cockles are consumed in abundance here, alongside albariño or godello wines from the region.

Madrid

Madrid is the crossroads of all regional cuisines in Spain. Culinary highlights include *tortilla de patata* from the restaurant Casa Dani and *cocido madrileño* (Madrid-Style Chickpea Stew, page 75) at Lhardy or La Bola. A typical way to end a long night out in Madrid or start the day off right is with *churros con chocolate* (Churros with Hot Chocolate, page 132) from Chocolatería San Ginés.

Valencia and Murcia

Murcia is the vegetable garden of Spain, with greenhouses that provide Spain and the rest of Europe with fresh produce throughout the year. Valencia's signature products are oranges and rice, such as Calasparra, a type of bomba rice, the main ingredient for the world-famous *paella valenciana*.

CHAPTER TWO

Tapas, Pintxos, and Other Small Plates

Small plates have swept the globe, and *pintxos* and tapas are the best ambassadors of this distinctive culinary wave. A pintxo is placed on a base such as bread or skewered, whereas a tapa is placed on a small plate and requires flatware. What follows are traditional, timeless recipes to enjoy with an aperitif, as a starter, light lunch, dinner, or brunch.

Garlic Shrimp (page 15)

Fair-Style Squid with Potatoes

CALAMARES Á FEIRA CON CACHELOS

Prep time: 5 minutes | Cook time: 30 minutes

Leaving Galicia without having *polbo á feira* (fair-style octopus) is impossible. The dish's aroma emanates from *pulperias*, restaurants that only serve dishes made with *pulpo* (octopus). This small plate is traditionally served on a round wooden dish with potatoes that have been boiled with the octopus, drizzled with olive oil, and seasoned with picante (hot) or sweet smoked paprika. This version uses squid, which is easier to find. Have a crusty loaf of bread? Use slices to soak up the paprika-seasoned oil. **SERVES 4**

6 medium Yukon Gold potatoes	1 bay leaf	Smoked paprika
1 pound calamari rings	1 teaspoon fine sea salt	Cayenne pepper
1 head garlic	Flaky sea salt	
	½ cup extra-virgin olive oil	

1. In a medium soup pot, combine the potatoes, calamari rings, whole head of garlic, bay leaf, fine sea salt, and enough cold water to cover. Bring to a boil over high heat and cook for 25 to 30 minutes, until the potatoes are fork-tender.

2. Drain well. (Discard the garlic and bay leaf.) Peel and slice the potatoes. Spread them on a platter and season with flaky sea salt. Scatter the calamari rings on top of the potatoes. Drizzle the olive oil over the calamari and potatoes. Sprinkle the paprika all over and season to taste with cayenne. Store leftovers in an airtight container in the refrigerator for up to 2 days.

MAKE IT MORE TRADITIONAL

This dish traditionally uses octopus. If you find vacuum-packed precooked octopus, prepare the potatoes as instructed above without the calamari. Pan-grill the octopus in olive oil in a cast-iron skillet, slice it, then distribute it over the potatoes. Season with flaky sea salt, the olive oil, paprika, and cayenne.

 WINE PAIRING

Pair this dish with an albariño from Rías Baixas or a young red of the mencia varietal from Bierzo.

Garlic Shrimp

GAMBAS AL AJILLO

Prep time: 35 minutes, plus up to 1 hour to marinate | Cook time: 10 minutes

This beloved shrimp dish is served in a *cazuela* (terra cotta casserole dish) with sizzling garlic oil and is topped off with sherry. To fully enjoy the garlic shrimp experience, dip your bread—*barquito* (little boat)—in the sauce and let it soak up these most representative flavors of Spain.

SERVES 4

---

1 ½ pounds medium shrimp, peeled, deveined, and rinsed

3 tablespoons sherry or dry white wine

Sea salt

Freshly ground black pepper

10 tablespoons extra-virgin olive oil, for shallow-frying

½ teaspoon red pepper flakes

1 teaspoon sherry vinegar

20 garlic cloves, sliced

1 parsley sprig, chopped

Bread, for serving

1. In a large bowl, combine the shrimp, sherry, and enough cold water to just barely cover. Set aside to marinate for at least 30 minutes or up to 1 hour. Drain the shrimp, reserving the liquid. Dry the shrimp with paper towels and season with salt and pepper.

2. Pour olive oil into a large sauté pan or skillet, add the pepper flakes, and heat over medium-low heat until hot. Add the garlic and cook for 3 minutes until lightly brown.

3. Add shrimp, 1 teaspoon of sherry vinegar, and 3 tablespoons of the reserved marinating liquid, and season with salt. Increase the heat to medium-high and cook for about 5 minutes, or until the shrimp turn a nice pink color and are just cooked through.

4. To serve, pour shrimp and garlic sauce into a bowl, garnish with the parsley, and serve with bread and a glass of white wine (see Wine Pairing). Store any leftovers in an airtight container in the refrigerator for up to 3 days.

MAKE IT MORE TRADITIONAL

Use a *cazuela* (terra cotta casserole dish) for a more authentic presentation. These can be purchased online in large or mini sizes.

 WINE PAIRING

A fruity wine of the albariño varietal from Rias Baixas or a chilled fino sherry from Jerez will pair nicely with this dish.

Tomato Toast

PAN AMB TOMÀQUET

Prep time: 15 minutes

Ideal for breakfast, snacks, appetizers, and tapas, this Spanish delicacy originated in Catalonia and is enjoyed all over Spain. It is easy to prepare and easy to customize. You can top it off with Serrano ham or prosciutto, anchovies, or olive oil–packed tuna, or be creative and build your *pintxo* on top of it. Try using campari tomatoes and a rustic bread. **SERVES 4**

4 tomatoes on the vine, halved	5 teaspoons extra-virgin olive oil, plus more for drizzling	8 slices rustic country-style bread
Fine sea salt		Flaky sea salt

1. Use the large holes of a box grater to grate the tomatoes into a bowl. Season to taste with fine sea salt and mix well. Add the olive oil and mix well with a fork or a whisk. (The tomato mixture can be stored in an airtight container in the refrigerator for up to 4 days.)

2. Toast the bread slices in a toaster or on a griddle until golden.

3. To serve, spoon the tomato mixture onto the toast. Sprinkle with flaky sea salt and drizzle with olive oil.

TECHNIQUE TIP

In a blender, combine 1½ cups cherry tomatoes, the olive oil, sea salt, and a couple of fresh basil leaves and blend until it reaches your desired consistency. Spoon this delicious sauce on little baguette toasts at a moment's notice.

REGIONAL VARIATION

In Catalonia, traditionally a garlic clove is rubbed onto the toast, and the tomato isn't grated but is also rubbed on the toast.

Crab Pintxo with Mayonnaise

PINTXO DE CHATKA CON MAYONESA

Prep time: 10 minutes, plus 10 minutes to chill

Pintxeando ("while eating *pintxos*") is a Basque saying that means "you share, you laugh, you debate, you enjoy"—in other words, you live life through magical small bites. Pintxos are to be enjoyed before lunch or dinner and end early. **SERVES 4**

---

1 pound lump crabmeat, shredded

1 cup mayonnaise, preferably homemade (see Aioli variation, page 40)

1 loaf ciabatta bread, cut into ¾-inch-thick slices

1 tablespoon finely chopped fresh chives

10 Little Gem lettuce leaves, separated and washed

Flaky sea salt

1 teaspoon sherry vinegar

2 tablespoons extra-virgin olive oil

1 teaspoon smoked paprika

1. In a bowl, mix together the crab and mayonnaise. Cover with plastic wrap and refrigerate for 20 to 30 minutes.

2. Place the ciabatta slices around the edges of a platter and top with the crab mixture. Garnish with the chives.

3. Place the lettuce leaves in the middle of the platter. Season the lettuce with sea salt and the vinegar, then drizzle with the olive oil. Sprinkle the whole platter with the smoked paprika and serve.

DIFFERENT SPIN

Place piquillo peppers on the bread before topping with the crab; swap out the crab for shrimp; top the crab with *asadillo de pimientos andaluz* (Roasted Pepper Salad from Andalucía, page 42); or garnish with grated hard-boiled egg on top. The bread can be served toasted or not.

 WINE PAIRING

When out for pintxos in the Basque Country, it is typical to order a *zurito*, a small lowball glass equivalent to half a beer in volume, filled with either a draft beer or wine. The beer is always a lighter draft beer similar to a pilsner, and the wine a Rueda verdejo, Rioja, or Ribera del Duero tempranillo.

Cured Ham Croquettes

CROQUETAS DE JAMÓN

Prep time: 10 minutes, plus 3 to 4 hours to chill | Cook time: 25 minutes

Croquetas are one of Spain's favorite small bites. They can be made out of whatever you have in the fridge, be it stew meat, fish, or veggies. The secret is the light, creamy béchamel. For a richer croquette, use 3 cups whole milk and ¼ cup heavy cream in the béchamel.

MAKES 40 TO 50 CROQUETTES

FOR THE BÉCHAMEL
8 tablespoons (1 stick)
   unsalted butter
1 medium yellow onion,
   finely chopped
Sea salt
Freshly ground white or
   black pepper

Pinch ground nutmeg
½ cup all-purpose flour
3¼ cups whole milk

FOR THE CROQUETTES
1 cup chopped prosciutto
¼ cup beef broth or
   chicken broth

4 large eggs
2 cups fine dried
   bread crumbs
Light, refined olive oil, for
   deep-frying

TO MAKE THE BÉCHAMEL

1. In a large nonstick sauté pan or skillet, melt the butter over medium heat. When very hot, add the onion and a pinch of salt and cook for about 5 minutes, until translucent.

2. Whisk in some pepper and the nutmeg, then slowly whisk in the flour and cook, whisking constantly to ensure there are no lumps of flour, for about 3 minutes.

3. Slowly add the milk and cook, whisking constantly, for about 3 minutes, until the sauce thickens. The béchamel is done when you can see the bottom of the pan as you draw a wooden spoon from one side to the other.

TO MAKE THE CROQUETTES

4. While whisking constantly, add the prosciutto to the béchamel, then slowly whisk in the broth and cook for 5 minutes, until the mixture bubbles.

5. Transfer the mixture to a 9-by-12-inch baking dish, cover with plastic wrap, and refrigerate until set, 3 to 4 hours.

6. Set up a dredging station: Beat the eggs in a shallow bowl. Spread the bread crumbs in a second shallow bowl. Line a large baking sheet with wax paper.

7. Scoop out tablespoon-size portions of the chilled croquette mixture and roll into 1-inch-long oblong balls. Dip a ball into the egg and then roll it in the bread crumbs until thoroughly coated. Place on the lined baking sheet. Repeat the process with the rest of the croquette mixture.

8. Pour about 2½ inches of olive oil into a deep but not wide pot. Heat the oil to between 340° and 350°F (check with a deep-fry thermometer).

9. Line a plate with paper towels. Working in small batches to avoid crowding, gently lower the croquettes into the oil and fry for about 1 minute, until they are a nice golden color. With a slotted spoon, transfer the croquettes to the paper towels to drain.

10. Arrange the croquettes on a serving plate and serve. Leftover, uncooked croquettes may be frozen flat in a resealable freezer bag or airtight container for up to 3 months. To reheat, thaw the frozen croquettes for 1 hour (they will still be partially frozen), then fry them as directed in steps 8 and 9.

MAKE IT MORE TRADITIONAL

Substitute cured Iberian ham or Serrano ham for the prosciutto. Or make the croquettes with chorizo, preferably Palacios brand Spanish chorizo (find it online).

 WINE PAIRING

A fruity and aromatic wine such as chardonnay, garnacha, or tempranillo is best to pair with a tapa of *croquetas*.

Bay Scallop Pie
EMPANADA DE ZAMBURIÑAS

Prep time: 15 minutes, plus 1 hour to rise | Cook time: 1 hour

This Galician pie is the iconic tapa of Spain's northwestern Celtic region and is found at many restaurants along the Santiago pilgrimage route. The pie can be as creative as you like, with a sautéed onion base and a filling of vegetables, meat, or seafood, including bay scallops, as here. The pie dough can be made of corn or wheat flour. If you use a premade pie crust, skip straight to making the filling. **SERVES 4**

FOR THE PIE DOUGH

1 (¼-ounce) packet active dry yeast

1 cup warm water (about 110°F)

1 pound (about 2 cups) all-purpose flour, plus more for dusting

1 large egg

1 teaspoon sea salt

½ cup extra-virgin olive oil, plus more for greasing the bowl

FOR THE PIE

½ cup extra-virgin olive oil

3 garlic cloves, finely chopped

¼ teaspoon red pepper flakes

1 yellow onion, finely chopped

1 teaspoon sea salt, plus more for seasoning

2 tablespoons finely chopped fresh parsley

1 red bell pepper, chopped

½ cup white wine

8 ounces bay scallops

1 teaspoon smoked paprika

All-purpose flour, for dusting

1 large egg, beaten

1 parsley sprig, for garnish

TO MAKE THE PIE DOUGH

1. In a small bowl, stir the yeast into the warm water just until dissolved. Set aside for about 2 minutes to hydrate the yeast.

2. Place the flour in a large bowl. Make a well in the middle of the flour. Crack the egg into the well. Add the yeast mixture, salt, and olive oil. Begin mixing the ingredients with a wooden spoon. As the dough starts to come together, switch to mixing with your hands. The dough should have a smooth, slightly sticky texture.

3. Dust a clean work surface with flour. Turn the dough out onto the surface and lightly dust the top with flour. Knead the dough for 5 to 10 minutes, until it springs back immediately when pressed with a finger.

4. Roll the dough into a ball. Grease a large bowl with olive oil. Place the dough in the bowl and cover with a clean kitchen towel. Place in a warm area and let rise until doubled in size, at least 1 hour but no more than 3 hours.

5. Preheat the oven to 390°F. Line a sheet pan with parchment paper.

6. In a medium sauté pan or skillet, heat the oil over medium heat. When hot, add the garlic and pepper flakes and stir. Add the onion and salt and sauté for 2 minutes, until the onions have softened. Reduce the heat to low, cover, and cook for 5 minutes. Add the parsley and bell pepper, increase the heat to medium, and cook for 10 minutes, until the peppers are firm-tender. Stir in the wine and cook, stirring occasionally, for 3 minutes to burn off the alcohol.

7. Season the scallops with salt, add to the pan, and cook for about 3 minutes, until opaque. Stir in the smoked paprika and cook for 3 minutes. Remove the pan from the heat and set aside to cool.

8. Lightly dust a work surface with flour. Divide the dough in half and form each half into a ball. Lightly dust a rolling pin with flour and roll each dough ball into a round or rectangle ⅛ to ¼ inch thick.

9. Place one of the dough rounds/rectangles on the prepared sheet pan. Spread half of the filling over the dough, leaving a generous 1-inch border. Gently place the second dough round/rectangle over the filling. Seal the pie by pinching the edges together gently between your thumb and index finger and slightly pulling the outer edge with each pinch. Brush the beaten egg over the top and edges of the dough. Using a sharp knife, cut three slits in the center of the dough.

10. Bake for 30 to 35 minutes, until the crust turns golden.

11. Remove the pie from the oven and let cool for 15 minutes. Place it on a large platter garnished with a sprig of parsley, ready to be cut and served. Store leftovers in an airtight container in the refrigerator for up to 3 days.

Spanish Potato Salad

ENSALADILLA RUSA

Prep time: 20 minutes, plus 30 minutes to chill | Cook time: 30 minutes

Ensaladilla rusa—Russian salad—is so named because it was originally made with partridge, smoked salmon, or caviar. The modern version—one of Spain's most popular and affordable tapas—is made with vegetables and albacore tuna. It's perfect to make ahead and serve chilled on a hot summer day. Decorate the salad with diced pimientos, boiled shrimp, or crabmeat. **SERVES 6**

2½ pounds Yukon Gold potatoes, peeled and quartered

3 carrots, peeled but whole

Fine sea salt

1 teaspoon extra-virgin olive oil

½ cup fresh or frozen green peas

8 hard-boiled eggs, divided

1 cup mayonnaise, preferably homemade (see Aioli variation, page 40)

½ cup Castelvetrano olives, pitted and chopped, plus 10 whole pitted olives

2 (6.7-ounce) cans olive oil–packed albacore tuna, drained

½ cup pepperoncini (optional)

1. In a large soup pot, combine the potatoes, carrots, 1 teaspoon salt, and water to cover. Bring to a boil over high heat. Reduce the heat to medium-low, cover, and cook for 25 to 30 minutes, until the potatoes are fork-tender. Drain and set aside to cool. When cool, dice the potatoes and carrots and place in a large bowl.

2. In a small skillet, heat the olive oil over medium heat. When hot, add the peas and sauté for 2 minutes, or until they warmed through. Season the peas with a pinch of salt and add to the bowl with the potatoes and carrots.

3. Chop 5 hard-boiled eggs and place in the bowl with the vegetables. Add ½ cup of the mayonnaise and 1 teaspoon salt and mix well. Add the chopped olives,

tuna, and remaining ½ cup mayonnaise and mix well. Taste and season with more salt if needed.

4. Grate the remaining 3 hard-boiled eggs. Garnish the potato salad with the grated eggs, whole pepperoncini (if using), and whole olives. Cover with plastic wrap and refrigerate for at least 30 minutes before serving, or refrigerate in an airtight container for up to 3 days.

DIFFERENT SPIN

If you have marinated roasted red peppers on hand, homemade or store-bought, you can garnish this salad with them. For a more authentic Spanish taste, swap the pepperoncini for *piparras* (Basque peppers in vinegar; see page 3), which you can easily find online.

 WINE PAIRING

Any refreshing summer beverage pairs well with this dish, such as a Lemon Summer Shandy (page 140) or Sangria (page 139).

Gildas (Mussel, Pepper, and Olive Skewers)

GILDAS DE MEJILLÓN

Prep time: 50 minutes, plus up to overnight to marinate | Cook time: 15 minutes

This *pintxo* was named in honor of Rita Hayworth's titular character in the 1946 Charles Vidor film *Gilda*, which was censored at the time in Spain. This green, spicy bite is crafted to emulate Rita's sexy and witty personality. Outside the Basque Country, it is known as a *banderilla*.
MAKES 20 SKEWERS

---

20 mussels (about 2 pounds), scrubbed and debearded

1 cup white wine

3 bay leaves, divided

1 cup extra-virgin olive oil, plus more for drizzling

2 garlic cloves, sliced

1 tablespoon smoked paprika

1 cup red wine vinegar

20 whole pepperoncini (about a 16-ounce jar)

20 Castelvetrano olives (about a 16-ounce jar), pitted

1. In large soup pot, combine the mussels, white wine, and 1 bay leaf. Cover the pot, place it over medium-high heat, and steam the mussels for about 3 minutes, or until the mussels open. Discard any mussels that do not open. Drain the mussels, reserving the cooking liquid. Remove the mussels from their shells and place in a bowl to cool.

2. In a medium sauté pan or skillet, heat the olive oil over medium-high heat. When hot, add the garlic and remaining 2 bay leaves. When the garlic is lightly browned, about 2 minutes, remove the pan from the heat. Quickly whisk in the smoked paprika. Add the vinegar and reserved mussel cooking liquid and mix well. It will bubble, so be careful not to burn yourself. Set aside to cool to room temperature.

3. Pour the cooled garlic oil over the mussels. Cover the bowl with plastic wrap and refrigerate to marinate the mussels for at least 45 minutes, or better yet overnight. (The longer you marinate them, the more pronounced the vinegar flavor will be.)

4. To serve, on each of 20 skewers, thread 1 pepperoncini, 1 mussel, 1 olive, and another mussel. Place the skewers on a plate and drizzle well with extra-virgin olive oil. Store any leftovers in an airtight container in the refrigerator for up to 3 days.

MAKE IT MORE TRADITIONAL

For a more authentic Gilda, swap the mussels for olive oil–packed Spanish anchovies from Cantabria or Catalonia and swap in *piparras* (Basque peppers) for the pepperoncini.

BEVERAGE PAIRING

This small bite pairs perfectly with a nice cold pilsner-style beer, a fino sherry, or vermouth.

Toasted Bread Crumbs from La Mancha

MIGAS MANCHEGAS

Prep time: 20 minutes, plus 2 hours to chill | Cook time: 50 minutes

Migas date back to the Al-Andalus years, when Muslims brought new methods of cooking with bread, enriching the Iberian Peninsula's food culture. *Migas manchegas* is a typical breakfast for hunters, perfect for warming up the body ahead of a long day outdoors. For brunch, top this bite with a fried or poached egg. **SERVES 4**

4 cups crusty French
   bread cubes

2 teaspoons fine sea salt

1½ cups water

4 tablespoons extra-virgin
   olive oil, divided

5 ounces pancetta, diced

1 link chorizo, diced

4 marinated sun-dried
   tomatoes, chopped

1 head garlic, separated into
   cloves and peeled

1 teaspoon smoked paprika

4 large eggs, for serving
   (optional)

1. Place the bread cubes in a large bowl. Dissolve the salt in the water and pour it over the bread. Mix gently. Place the bread on a clean kitchen towel and wrap it. Then return the bundle to the same bowl, moving the bundle around in the bowl to distribute the moisture evenly. Place the bowl in the refrigerator for at least 2 hours or overnight.

2. In a large skillet, heat 1 tablespoon of olive oil over medium heat. When hot, add the pancetta and cook for 5 minutes, or until crispy. Add the chorizo and sun-dried tomatoes and cook for 3 minutes, until well browned. Drain off any grease and set aside in a bowl.

3. In the same skillet, heat the remaining 3 tablespoons of olive oil. When hot, add the garlic cloves and paprika and cook for about 2 minutes to brown. If you choose, you can leave the garlic in the pan and proceed to the next step. Or, using a slotted spoon, remove the garlic.

4. Add some of the bread to the pan without crowding the bread cubes. Increase the heat to medium-high and sauté, stirring constantly to prevent from burning, remove moisture, and lightly toast. As the bread begins to toast, add more bread. Toasting all the bread will take about 30 minutes.

5. Add the chorizo/pancetta/sun-dried tomato mixture to the pan and stir until all of the ingredients are mixed together, about 5 minutes.

6. If desired, fry or poach the eggs and serve on top of the toasted bread crumbs.

DIFFERENT SPIN

Try adding sweet raisins and grapes to contrast this dish's saltiness. Add the raisins with the sun-dried tomatoes in step 2. Use the grapes as a garnish.

 WINE PAIRING

This dish pairs well with a cava or with a Rioja of the tempranillo, graciano, or mazuelo varietal.

Fierce Potatoes
PATATAS BRAVAS

Prep time: 15 minutes | Cook time: 35 minutes

It's not clear if *patatas bravas* originated at Casa Pellico or at La Casona, two bars in Madrid that no longer exist. What is remembered is that the bars' long entry lines were due to this dish. There's controversy over whether the authentic sauce contains tomatoes, which this recipe calls for. Many bars in Madrid serve this dish with Aioli (page 40) instead.
SERVES 4

---

6 Yukon gold
  potatoes, peeled

3 teaspoons fine sea salt,
  divided, plus more for
  seasoning

¼ cup olive oil

1 medium yellow
  onion, sliced

2 garlic cloves,
  finely chopped

1 teaspoon red
  pepper flakes

1 tablespoon
  smoked paprika

1 cup Spanish Tomato
  Sauce (page 59)

¾ cup chicken broth or
  vegetable broth

2 tablespoons sherry vinegar

3 to 4 cups olive oil,
  for frying

Freshly ground
  black pepper

1. Roughly cut the potatoes into irregular 1-inch chunks.

2. Fill a medium soup pot with enough water to cover the potatoes, add 2 teaspoons of salt, and bring to a boil over high heat. Add the potatoes and 2 teaspoons of the salt and cook for 5 to 7 minutes, until the potatoes are almost but not fully cooked (this will help achieve a moist and cooked interior after they are fried). Drain the potatoes, dry them well, and set aside.

3. In a medium sauté pan or skillet, heat the olive oil over medium heat. When hot, add the onion, garlic, and remaining 1 teaspoon salt and mix well. Cover, reduce the heat to medium-low, and cook for 5 minutes to soften the onion. Uncover and cook for 10 minutes, until the onion is soft and translucent. Stir in the pepper flakes and smoked paprika.

4. Stir in the tomato sauce and cook for 2 minutes. Add the broth, bring to a simmer, then reduce the heat to low and cook for 3 minutes to reduce a bit. Stir in the vinegar. Transfer the sauce to a blender or food processor and blend for 3 to 4 minutes, until it has a creamy texture. Set aside.

5. Pour about 2½ inches of olive oil into a heavy pot. Heat over medium-high heat to 350°F (test with a deep-fry thermometer).

6. Line a plate with paper towels. Working in batches to avoid crowding, fry the potatoes for 10 minutes, until golden and crispy. Use a slotted spoon to transfer the potatoes to the paper towel–lined plate. Sprinkle with salt and black pepper while still hot.

7. Serve in a bowl with the sauce drizzled on top.

BEVERAGE PAIRING

Pair with a refreshing beverage to put out the fire, such as a beer, a rosé from Navarra, or a rosé cava.

Moorish Pork Loin Skewers

PINCHO MORUNO

Prep time: 10 minutes, plus 30 minutes to marinate | Cook time: 15 minutes

The Moorish skewer is popular in Ceuta and Melilla, tiny Spanish enclaves on the northern shores of Morocco, where you can enjoy them with *té moruno*, a Moroccan green tea with mint. The skewers also appear in bars throughout Spain, sometimes made with lamb or chicken but mostly with pork. For the best flavor, marinate these skewers overnight. **SERVES 4**

FOR THE MARINADE

10 garlic cloves, peeled

¼ cup ground cumin

10 saffron threads

2 small yellow onions, finely chopped

8 tablespoons fresh lemon juice, divided

5 tablespoons smoked paprika

½ teaspoon ground cinnamon

6 cilantro sprigs, finely chopped

2 teaspoons sea salt

½ teaspoon freshly ground black pepper

1 cup extra-virgin olive oil

FOR THE SKEWERS

2 pounds pork loin, cut into 1-inch cubes

¼ cup extra-virgin olive oil

Flaky sea salt

1 cilantro sprig, for garnish

1 lemon, halved, for serving

TO MAKE THE MARINADE

1. Place the garlic, cumin, and saffron in the blender to create a paste.

2. Set aside 1 cup of the marinade to heat and serve as a sauce. In a medium bowl, mix together the onions and 2 tablespoons of the lemon juice, coating thoroughly. Add the garlic mixture, smoked paprika, cinnamon, cilantro, salt, pepper, olive oil, and remaining 6 tablespoons lemon juice. Mix well.

TO MAKE THE SKEWERS

3. In a medium bowl, combine the pork and the marinade and stir to coat. Set the remaining marinade aside. Cover the pork with plastic wrap and refrigerate for at least 30 minutes, or up to overnight.

4. Thread the pork onto 8-inch skewers.

5. In a 12-inch cast-iron skillet, heat the olive oil over high heat until hot. Working in batches, add the skewers of pork in a single layer and cook for 3 minutes. Flip and cook for 3 minutes more, or until cooked through. The marinade will keep the skewers moist and juicy as they cook.

6. In a small saucepan, heat the reserved marinade until hot.

7. Arrange the skewers on a plate and sprinkle with flaky sea salt. Drizzle the warmed sauce on top of the skewers. Garnish with a sprig of cilantro and the lemon halves. Store any leftovers in an airtight container in the refrigerator for up to 3 days.

DIFFERENT SPINS

Lamb, boneless chicken, or beef can be substituted for the pork loin. For a spicier Moorish skewer, add a pinch of cayenne pepper. In Spain, this is done with picante (hot) paprika.

BEVERAGE PAIRING

To be the most authentic, the skewers should be served with Moroccan green tea with mint, but they also pair well with a tempranillo crianza, aged in oak for 12 months.

Cod Brandade with Toast

TOSTADAS CON BRANDADA DE BACALAO

Prep time: 10 minutes | Cook time: 20 minutes

This tapa can be served in a bowl with toast or spread over Tomato Toast (page 16) and served "au gratin." It can be the used as the base for many *pintxos*, including pintxos of brandade, piquillo peppers, and quince paste or brandade, microgreens, and figs. Invent your own enticing combination. *Buen provecho (bon appétit)*! **SERVES 6**

---

1 cup extra-virgin olive oil

4 garlic cloves, sliced

1¼ pounds rock cod fillets

2 pinches ground nutmeg

Salt and pepper to taste

⅔ cup whole milk, at room temperature

1 baguette, cut into ¾-inch-thick slices

2 tablespoons finely chopped fresh parsley

1. In a medium sauté pan or skillet, heat the olive oil over medium heat. When hot, add the garlic and cook for 2 minutes, or until lightly browned. Using a skimmer or slotted spoon, remove the garlic slices (before they turn dark brown) and set them aside.

2. Line a plate with paper towels. Cut cod fillets in half. Place the cod in the pan and cook for 2 minutes on each side, until opaque. Remove the pan from the heat, cover, and let sit for 5 minutes to finish cooking. Using a skimmer or slotted spoon, transfer the cod to the paper towel–lined plate to drain. Do not discard the oil in the pan.

3. Using a mortar and pestle, crush the cod into a paste with a pinch of nutmeg. You may have to do this in small chunks depending on how big your mortar is. Remove and discard any fish bones you find.

4. In a small saucepan, combine the milk and a pinch of nutmeg. Bring it just to a simmer over medium heat, then remove from the heat.

5. Transfer the crushed cod to a blender. Add salt and pepper to taste. With the blender running on low speed, slowly add the reserved oil from the pan, little by little. The cod will have a paste-like consistency. Next, add the hot milk little by little, letting the fish paste absorb it. Place the brandade in a bowl and set the bowl on a serving platter.

6. Toast the baguette slices in the oven or toaster.

7. Serve the brandade surrounded by the toasts. Top the brandade with the lightly browned garlic and the parsley. Store leftover brandade in an airtight container in the refrigerator for up to 3 days.

REGIONAL VARIATION

Brandade recipes from the Basque Country tend to include potato, which helps to thicken the brandade. To incorporate potato into this recipe, peel 1 russet potato and cut into medium dice. Boil it in salted water until fork-tender. Add the potato to the blender with the crushed cod in step 5 and proceed with the recipe.

 WINE PAIRING

Brandade pairs well with Manzanilla sherry or a chilled Txacoli. A verdejo or ribeiro white wine will also pair well with it.

Fried Calamari

RABAS DE CALAMAR

Prep time: 5 minutes | Cook time: 15 minutes

Una de rabas is a typical phrase heard in bars in the Spanish city of Santander. It means "Waiter, give me a plate of calamari." It might be the Cantabrian breeze or the way the rabas are cut into strips that makes enjoying the dish in this region exceptionally delightful. The breading may differ from bar to bar: Some use a batter of eggs and flour, while others use half bread and half flour. In Santander, calamari are always coated with seasoned flour. **SERVES 4**

---

2 cups all-purpose flour

2 teaspoons sea salt, plus more for seasoning

½ teaspoon ground white pepper

1 pound squid, cleaned, bodies cut lengthwise into ½-inch-wide strips, tentacles kept separate

Refined olive oil, for deep-frying

1 lemon, cut into wedges, for serving

Aioli (page 40) or Spicy Mojo Sauce (page 51), for serving

1. In a large bowl, mix together the flour, salt, and white pepper. Add the squid, a few pieces at a time, and toss until fully coated.

2. Pour 3 inches of oil into a deep pot and heat to 340° to 350°F (test with a deep-fry thermometer). Reduce the heat under the pot as needed to maintain the temperature of the oil.

3. Line a plate with paper towels. Working in batches, gently drop the squid into the oil and fry for 3 to 5 minutes, until golden brown. With a slotted spoon or tongs, transfer to the paper towel–lined plate to drain. Season with salt while hot.

4. Serve hot on a big plate or in individual bowls with the lemon wedges and aioli or mojo alongside.

SUBSTITUTION

Instead of a whole squid, you can use frozen calamari rings. Thaw the rings before using.

 WINE PAIRING

Enjoy the calamari with a verdejo from Rueda or a young white wine of the malvasia varietal from Lanzarote.

Marinated Shellfish Salad

SALPICÓN DE MARISCOS

Prep time: 15 minutes, plus 1 hour to marinate

This tapa is especially common in Andalucía, where shellfish and olive oil are plentiful. Enjoy it chilled over lettuce as a light summer dinner, as an appetizer for a special celebration, or in a martini glass or on a tartlet as a passed hors d'oeuvre for a cocktail party. **SERVES 4**

½ cup fresh lemon juice

6 tablespoons extra-virgin olive oil

2 tablespoons fino sherry or port

2 pinches flaky sea salt

⅛ teaspoon ground white pepper

½ sweet yellow onion, finely chopped

4 tomatoes on the vine

1 pound cooked shrimp, peeled, deveined, and cut into ½-inch pieces

1. In a large bowl, whisk together the lemon juice, olive oil, and sherry. Add the salt, white pepper, and onion and mix well.

2. Using a serrated knife, peel the tomatoes. Cut them in half and remove the seeds. Finely chop. Add to the bowl with the onion and mix well.

3. Stir the shrimp into the bowl. Cover the bowl with plastic wrap and refrigerate for at least 1 hour, or up to (preferably) 6 hours.

4. Serve the salad in its bowl or portion it into champagne coupes or martini glasses. Store any leftovers in an airtight container in the refrigerator for up to 3 days.

REGIONAL VARIATIONS

This recipe varies immensely from bar to bar or family to family, using crab, mussels, clams, or even lobster instead of shrimp. Some variations add finely chopped red and green bell peppers.

 WINE PAIRING

This refreshing dish, with its sweetness and acidity, pairs well with a sauvignon blanc.

Spanish Potato and Onion Frittata
TORTILLA ESPAÑOLA

Prep time: 20 minutes | Cook time: 40 minutes

Most of Spain loves a *tortilla*, perfect for any meal: breakfast, midmorning snack, lunch, or dinner. It is one of Spanish cuisine's most symbolic dishes. Casa Dani in Madrid's Mercado de la Paz serves tortillas by the hundreds to the locals and is considered the best tortilla in town by many. Although making a tortilla is a bit labor-intensive, every bite makes it worth the effort! **SERVES 6**

---

9 large eggs

3 tablespoons extra-virgin olive oil

1 medium yellow onion, thinly sliced

1 teaspoon fine sea salt

2 to 3 cups grapeseed oil

7 medium Yukon Gold potatoes, peeled and thinly sliced

Sliced tomato or Roasted Pepper Salad from Andalucía (page 42), for serving

1. In a large bowl, beat the eggs. Set aside.

2. In an 8- to 10-inch nonstick skillet (make sure you have a plate that will fit fully over the skillet), heat the olive oil over low heat. When hot, add the onion and salt and sauté for 2 minutes, until the onion softens. Cover the pan with a lid and cook for 5 minutes. Uncover and cook for 10 to 15 minutes, until translucent. Drain the onion and add it to the bowl with the eggs.

3. In the same pan, heat 1½ inches of grapeseed oil over medium heat. When it is hot, work in batches to fry the potatoes until they are cooked through, 12 to 15 minutes. As you work, use a skimmer to transfer the fried potatoes to a colander to drain, then add them to the bowl with the eggs. Add more oil to the pan as needed between batches, heating the oil until hot before adding the potatoes. Between batches, press the potatoes and onions into the eggs with a whisk, binding them together. This will add texture to your finished tortilla.

4. Once all the potatoes are fried, drain off most of the oil remaining in the pan, leaving just enough so it is well greased. Place the pan over medium heat and add the potato-egg mixture. Cook, gently shaking the pan occasionally, for 5 minutes, or until the underside and edges are set and lightly browned.

Run a spatula around the egg to loosen it, then invert a plate over the pan (so it's bottom-side up). With your hand holding the plate in place, carefully flip the pan over so the tortilla falls out onto the plate. Place the pan back on the burner and slide the tortilla, uncooked-side down, back into the pan. Cook for 2 to 3 minutes, until the bottom is set and lightly browned. When you shake the pan, the tortilla should not wobble. Flip the tortilla one more time and cook until the bottom is a darker brown.

5. Serve immediately on the same plate used to flip the tortilla, with a sliced tomato or roasted pepper salad. Store any remaining tortilla on a small plate covered with plastic wrap in the refrigerator to enjoy the following day for breakfast.

TECHNIQUE TIP
A hinged frittata pan will facilitate your tortilla flipping. Frittata pans have lids that latch on so that you can easily flip the contents of the pan. When using a plate to flip the tortilla, it's very important that the plate fully cover the pan so that you can safely flip it.

BEVERAGE PAIRING
A nice cold pilsner-style beer pairs best with tortilla, or try it with a young tempranillo or fino sherry.

CHAPTER THREE

Sides, Salads, and Sauces

A three-course meal in Spain starts with a soup, vegetable dish, or stew, followed by an entrée and side dishes such as potatoes and roasted peppers or a salad. Although Spaniards use sauces sparingly, a few are a must, such as aioli, romesco sauce, and mojo sauce—all of which you'll find in this chapter, along with several wonderful side dishes and salads.

Mixed Salad (page 45)

Aioli

ALIOLI

Prep time: 5 minutes

Aioli is a traditional Mediterranean sauce with a zesty garlic punch that complements rice and noodle dishes, fish, poultry, grilled meat, and vegetables. It was originally made with just sliced garlic, salt, and olive oil, crushed and stirred in a mortar with a pestle until it emulsified. Today, a stick blender speeds this process up. You can use olive oil, vegetable oil, or a combination of both. Using only olive oil will give the aioli a stronger taste. **MAKES 1½ CUPS**

---

1 large egg at room
 temperature

2 garlic cloves, minced or
 pressed in a garlic press
2 cups sunflower oil

½ teaspoon fine sea salt
½ teaspoon fresh
 lemon juice

1. Place the egg, garlic, oil, and salt in a medium bowl in the order listed.

2. Add the lemon juice after the mixture begins to emulsify. Place a stick blender on top of the egg and begin to blend, without moving the blender, until the mixture emulsifies. Once you see it has emulsified, you can gently move the blender up and down to finish blending to a mayonnaise consistency.

3. Transfer the aioli to a bowl and cover with plastic wrap. Refrigerate until ready to serve, or store in an airtight container in the refrigerator for up to 2 days.

TECHNIQUE TIP

If the aioli does not emulsify into a mayonnaise-like consistency, place 1 egg in a similar size bowl as the one you started with. Place the blender directly over the yolk and, before blending, add one-third of the previous recipe to the bowl. Start the blender and hold it without moving it until the egg mixture emulsifies. Then proceed to slowly add the remaining original mixture while raising the blender up and down.

DIFFERENT SPIN

Mayonnaise is simply aioli without garlic. Follow the recipe as written but omit the garlic.

Grilled Calçots

CALÇOTS

Prep time: 5 minutes | Cook time: 10 minutes

A *calçot* is a scallion-like onion typically eaten in Catalonia from November until April. At the end of the season, there is a beloved annual tradition in Vals, Tarragona, called a *calçotada*. At this festival, the onions are char-grilled over vine shoots and served wrapped in newspaper with bowls of Romesco Sauce (page 54) accompanied by *botifarras* (sausages), white Catalan beans, and local wines. **SERVES 6**

---

30 large scallions or spring onions	¼ cup extra-virgin olive oil	Flaky sea salt
	1 teaspoon fine sea salt	

1. Remove the outer layers of the scallions and cut off the root ends. Slice them in half lengthwise.

2. In a large heavy skillet (preferably cast iron for the best char), heat the olive oil and fine sea salt over high heat, stirring to dissolve the salt. When very hot, working in batches, add the scallions in a single layer and cook until charred on the first side, 2 to 3 minutes; they should be almost burnt on the outside and juicy on the inside. Flip and char the second side. Season with salt.

3. Serve the scallions on a platter. Store leftovers in an airtight container in the refrigerator for up to 2 days.

MAKE IT MORE TRADITIONAL

To prepare the scallions as is done at a calçotada, grill them on an outdoor grill, and once they are done, keep them warm by wrapping them in aluminum foil (though traditionally this would be done with newspaper).

 WINE PAIRING

This dish pairs well with a tempranillo, garnacha, or merlot.

Roasted Pepper Salad from Andalucía

ASADILLO DE PIMIENTOS ANDALUZ

Prep time: 15 minutes | Cook time: 45 minutes

Asadillo de pimientos andaluz is a dish representative of the Mediterranean but is popular in many cities and regions throughout Spain. It's made with just three main ingredients: red bell peppers, extra-virgin olive oil, and sea salt. It's a flavorful, well-loved dish that is great to eat cold as a tapa or a salad or to accompany fish, meat, lamb chops, or rabbit. **SERVES 4**

---

4 tomatoes on the vine

4 red bell peppers

5 tablespoons extra-virgin olive oil, divided

Sea salt

3 garlic cloves, sliced

½ teaspoon red pepper flakes

½ teaspoon ground cumin

1 tablespoon balsamic vinegar

1. Postion a rack in the center of the oven and preheat the broiler.

2. Using a sharp knife, cut a small "X" on the bottoms of the tomatoes. Rub all sides of the bell peppers and tomatoes with 2 tablespoons of the olive oil. Place the peppers and tomatoes in a baking pan large enough to hold them. Roast the vegetables for 30 minutes, 15 minutes on each side. Remove the pan from the oven, cover it with aluminum foil, and let the peppers and tomatoes cool on the pan.

3. When cool, remove the peppers and tomatoes, reserving the liquid in the pan. Carefully peel and seed the bell peppers. Cut the flesh into long strips and set aside in a large bowl with the reserved liquid from the baking pan.

4. Peel the tomatoes and remove the seeds. Place the flesh in a blender, add salt to taste, and blend until smooth. Set aside.

5. In a medium sauté pan or skillet, heat the remaining 3 tablespoons olive oil over medium heat. When hot, add the garlic and pepper flakes and brown for 1 minute. Add the roasted pepper slices and any liquid in the bowl, the blended tomatoes, cumin, and salt to taste and mix well. Reduce the heat to medium-low and cook for 15 minutes, until the sauce thickens and reduces some, shaking the pan from time to time.

6. Stir in the balsamic vinegar, remove the pan from the heat, and let cool.

7. Transfer to a bowl and serve at room temperature. Store any leftovers in an airtight container in the refrigerator for 3 to 5 days.

REGIONAL VARIATION

In Andalucía, only red bell peppers are used, but in other regions, green bell peppers and eggplant may be added. The *asadillo* can be garnished with olives or capers.

Little Gems and Toasted Garlic Salad

COGOLLOS DE TUDELA

Prep time: 10 minutes

Little Gems are a type of lettuce, and the best ones are grown in Tudela, Navarra, in Spain. Try this salad when Little Gems are in season, and when they are not, make it with chopped romaine lettuce. **SERVES 4**

---

4 heads Little Gem lettuce

1 cup plus 3 tablespoons extra-virgin olive oil (preferably Arbequina), divided

2 garlic cloves, minced

Flaky sea salt

2 tablespoons red wine vinegar

1. Quarter each head of lettuce through the stem to form triangular wedges. Place the wedges cut-side up in a spoke pattern on a large serving plate.

2. In a small skillet, heat 3 tablespoons of the olive oil over medium-low heat. When hot, add the garlic and cook for 1 to 2 minutes to very lightly brown, being careful not to burn it. Sprinkle the toasted garlic over the lettuce wedges.

3. Sprinkle some salt over the lettuce, followed by the vinegar, and then drizzle with the remaining ½ cup olive oil.

REGIONAL VARIATION

In the Basque Country, this salad might be topped with olive oil–packed albacore tuna (*bonito del norte*) and a red bell pepper and scallion vinaigrette. Finely chop ½ small red bell pepper, 4 scallions, and ⅓ cup chopped, pitted green olives. Add ½ cup extra-virgin olive oil and ¼ cup sherry vinegar and season with salt. Let macerate for 20 minutes, then pour the vinaigrette over the salad.

 WINE PAIRING

This dish pairs well with a light Rioja viura that hasn't been aged in oak and has lemon, citrus fruit, and floral aromas.

Mixed Salad

ENSALADA MIXTA

Prep time: 20 minutes | Cook time: 25 minutes

Ensalada mixta is the Spanish version of a Niçoise salad. It is a simple and flavorful dish typically found on menus as a starter. There are many slight variations on the theme, including adding corn. No matter the version, it is always made with a simple vinaigrette. **SERVES 4**

Fine sea salt

2 medium Yukon Gold potatoes

4 asparagus spears, woody ends trimmed

1 head red-leaf lettuce, chopped

1 tomato on the vine, cut into wedges

4 large hard-boiled eggs, peeled and cut into wedges

½ sweet onion, thinly sliced

16 Castelvetrano olives

8 ounces olive oil–packed albacore tuna (preferably Ortiz bonito del norte), drained

Flaky sea salt

¼ cup sherry vinegar

¾ cup extra-virgin olive oil (preferably Arbequina)

1. In a medium pot, bring enough water to cover the potatoes and a pinch of salt to a boil over medium-high heat. Add the whole potatoes and cook for 25 minutes, until fork-tender. Drain the potatoes and let cool, then peel and slice them.

2. Set up a bowl of salted ice water. Cook the asparagus in a steamer basket for 5 minutes, or until crisp-tender. Plunge the asparagus into the ice bath. Drain and pat dry.

3. In a large bowl, toss the lettuce, sliced potatoes, tomato wedges, asparagus, eggs, onion, olives, and tuna.

4. Sprinkle the salad with flaky sea salt, then drizzle with the vinegar, followed by the olive oil. It is important to dress the salad in this order, as the oil will seal in the salt and vinegar. Mix well and serve.

MAKE IT MORE TRADITIONAL

This recipe traditionally calls for canned white asparagus and sometimes corn. In Spain, many people like to add corn, which is excellent charred.

Grilled Asparagus
ESPÁRRAGOS TRIGUEROS A LA PLANCHA

Prep time: 5 minutes | Cook time: 12 minutes

Asparagus is a key ingredient in Spanish cuisine. You will find it scrambled in eggs, included in rice dishes and in vegetable mélanges, sautéed with Serrano ham, in a tapa, or on a salad. Here it's grilled in a cast-iron skillet with extra-virgin olive oil and flaky sea salt—simple, easy, and natural! **SERVES 6**

---

3 tablespoons extra-virgin olive oil

1 teaspoon flaky sea salt, plus more for seasoning

24 to 30 asparagus spears, woody ends trimmed

¼ cup water

Homemade mayonnaise or Aioli (page 40)

½ lemon

1. Pour the olive oil into a large cast-iron skillet and stir in the salt. Set over high heat and once hot, place the asparagus spears in the skillet in a single layer. Reduce the heat to medium and cook for 5 minutes, until the tips turn crisp. Turn the asparagus over and add the water and a pinch of salt. Cook the asparagus, turning them from time to time, until the water evaporates and they are cooked to your desired tenderness, about 5 minutes.

2. Serve on a large platter with mayonnaise or aioli. Finish with a sprinkle of salt and a squeeze of lemon juice. Store leftovers in an airtight container in the refrigerator for up to 2 days.

REGIONAL VARIATION

At Taberna Laredo in Madrid, the asparagus is served with diced heirloom tomatoes and shaved Parmesan cheese.

Spinach with Raisins and Pine Nuts

ESPINACAS CON PASAS Y PIÑONES

Prep time: 5 minutes | Cook time: 15 minutes

This is a typical side dish in Catalonia that's also known as *espinacas a la catalana*. It is believed that spinach was brought to Europe in the Middle Ages by Muslims who began to cultivate it in Seville. They grew it especially for its medicinal properties, as it was believed to be anti-inflammatory and purgative. This dark, leafy green is rich in vitamins and minerals and is part of the Mediterranean diet. **SERVES 4**

---

3 tablespoons extra-virgin olive oil

2 garlic cloves, minced

½ cup pine nuts

3 tablespoons raisins

2 pounds fresh spinach, tough stems trimmed

Sea salt

1. In a medium sauté pan or skillet, heat the olive oil over medium heat. When hot, add the garlic and cook for 1 to 2 minutes, until golden. Stir in the pine nuts, then the raisins, and sauté for 2 minutes.

2. Add half of the spinach to the pan. Cover and cook for about 2 minutes, until it wilts and reduces in volume. Add the remaining spinach, cover, and cook until it wilts. Season with salt. Reduce the heat to a simmer and cook for 5 to 8 minutes, until the liquid released by the spinach has evaporated.

3. Serve hot. Store any leftovers in an airtight container in the refrigerator for up to 3 days.

REGIONAL VARIATIONS

Spaniards love cured pork, so many recipes include ¼ cup chopped Serrano ham, which would be added after the pine nuts and raisins. There are also variations where sliced almonds are subbed in for half the pine nuts, or ½ teaspoon smoked paprika is added, or 1 onion, finely chopped, is included when sautéing the garlic.

Vegetable Mélange

MENESTRA DE VERDURAS

Prep time: 15 minutes | Cook time: 30 minutes

This recipe is typical in northern Spain, especially in Navarra, the garden of the Basque Country. It is usually served during the spring or summer with seasonal vegetables as a starter or as an entrée topped with two poached eggs. You may also find it garnished with fried breaded artichokes. Use any of your favorite seasonal vegetables. This dish is also nice when garnished with sliced hard-boiled or poached eggs. **SERVES 4**

10 asparagus spears, woody ends trimmed

Fine sea salt

1 pound green beans, trimmed and cut into thirds

1 cup green peas

4 carrots, diced

8 frozen artichoke hearts, thawed and patted dry

8 ounces frozen shelled edamame, thawed

12 small broccoli florets

2 medium Yukon Gold potatoes, peeled and cut into medium-small pieces

¼ cup extra-virgin olive oil

3 garlic cloves, chopped

1 small yellow onion, finely chopped

Freshly ground black pepper

½ cup diced Serrano ham or prosciutto

1 tablespoon all-purpose flour (optional)

1. Cut each spear of asparagus crosswise on an angle into 4 pieces.

2. Line a platter with paper towels. In a large soup pot, bring enough water to cover the vegetables and 1 teaspoon salt to a boil over medium-high heat. Add the green beans, peas, carrots, and asparagus and boil for 5 to 8 minutes, until tender. Using a slotted spoon or skimmer, transfer the vegetables to the paper towel–lined platter.

3. To the boiling water, add the artichokes, edamame, and broccoli and boil for 3 minutes, then transfer to the platter.

4. Add the potatoes to the pot and boil for 15 to 20 minutes, until fork-tender. Transfer to the platter, reserving the liquid in the pot.

5. Meanwhile, in a large skillet, heat the olive oil over medium heat. When hot, add the garlic and onion and season with salt and pepper. Cook for 15 minutes, or until the onion is soft and translucent.

6. Add the ham to the pan and sauté for 2 minutes.

7. For a thicker sauce, place the flour in a small bowl and stir in ¼ cup of the reserved vegetable cooking water, then pour this slurry into the skillet. Cook, stirring, for 2 minutes to remove the raw flavor of the flour.

8. Add 1 cup of the reserved vegetable cooking water to the pan and mix well. Reduce the heat to low and simmer for 10 minutes.

9. Add the vegetables and potatoes to the pan and mix well. Add 1 cup of the reserved vegetable cooking water and mix well. Cover and simmer over low heat for 5 minutes to reduce the liquid somewhat.

10. Serve on a large platter as a side dish. Store leftovers in an airtight container in the refrigerator for up to 3 days.

 WINE PAIRING
This dish pairs well with an oak-aged verdejo or chardonnay.

Fava Beans with Ham

HABITAS CON JAMÓN

Prep time: 10 minutes | Cook time: 20 minutes

Fava beans are typical of dishes in Granada, as the beans are cultivated in its fertile valley. A tradition of the region's food culture is to eat fresh favas with *saladillas* (round bread made with olive oil and sea salt) and salt cod. At the bars in Granada, a great treat is a *bocadillo* (sandwich) made with sautéed fava beans and onions and a slice of cured Iberian or Serrano ham on a baguette. **SERVES 4**

¼ cup extra-virgin olive oil

1 small yellow onion, finely chopped

2 garlic cloves, sliced

½ cup chopped Serrano ham or prosciutto

1 pound peeled shelled fresh fava beans (see Tip) or frozen shelled edamame, thawed

½ cup water

Flaky sea salt

1. In a medium sauté pan or skillet, heat the olive oil over medium heat. When hot, add the onion and garlic and sauté for 5 minutes, until soft and translucent.

2. Add the ham and sauté for 5 minutes.

3. Add the beans and cook, stirring, to coat with the onion and garlic, for about 2 minutes. Add the water and cook for 5 minutes, then reduce the heat to a simmer and cook for 15 minutes, until the beans are tender and the liquid has reduced.

4. Season the dish with salt and serve. Store leftovers in an airtight container in the refrigerator for 3 to 5 days.

TECHNIQUE TIP

If you're making this with fresh fava beans, you need to buy 2 to 2½ pounds in the pod to get 1 pound shelled. After shelling the beans, blanch them in boiling water, drain, rinse to cool, then peel off their thick skins.

BEVERAGE PAIRING

Enjoy this dish as they do in Granada, with a nice cold pilsner-style beer.

Spicy Mojo Sauce
MOJO PICÓN

Prep time: 15 minutes

Mojo picón is the "salsa" of the Canary Islands, and it is found on every table throughout the archipelago. It pairs beautifully with *papas arrugadas* (wrinkled potatoes), as well as with beef. The word *mojo* is derived from the Portuguese word *molho*, which means "sauce," as many of the original settlers of the Canary Islands were from Madeira, a Portuguese island. **SERVES 6**

---

4 garlic cloves, coarsely chopped

2 tomatoes on the vine, peeled (see Tip) and chopped

1 red bell pepper, coarsely chopped

1 teaspoon sea salt

1 teaspoon ground cumin

1 teaspoon smoked paprika

¼ teaspoon red pepper flakes

½ cup vegetable oil

In a blender, combine the garlic, tomatoes, bell pepper, salt cumin, paprika, pepper flakes, and oil and blend on high speed for 10 to 15 minutes, until the sauce has a creamy texture. Store in an airtight container in the refrigerator for up to 4 days.

TECHNIQUE TIP

To peel tomatoes: Set up a bowl of ice and water. Using a sharp knife, cut a small "X" on the bottom of each tomato. Place the tomatoes in a medium saucepan and pour boiling water over them to cover. Blanch the tomatoes for 50 seconds, until the skins soften, which will make them easier to peel. Using tongs, transfer the tomatoes to the ice bath to stop the cooking. When cool enough to handle, pull the skin off the tomatoes.

REGIONAL VARIATION

Mojo verde is the green mojo of the Canary Islands. To make it, in a blender, combine 8 garlic cloves, 1 bunch cilantro, 1 teaspoon ground cumin, salt to taste, ¼ cup white wine vinegar, and ¾ cup extra-virgin olive oil and blend to a creamy texture.

Baker's Potatoes

PATATAS PANADERAS

Prep time: 10 minutes | Cook time: 1 hour

The name "baker's potatoes" dates to an era when home ovens were uncommon, so Spaniards brought their roasts to the local baker to cook and always asked for the "baker's potatoes" to accompany the meat. In Andalucía, they are known as poor man's potatoes because they were made with whatever you had left in the pantry, which was not a lot during post–Spanish Civil War times. They are delicious with roasted lamb and fish or with fried eggs and chorizo. **SERVES 4**

4 medium Yukon Gold potatoes, peeled and thinly sliced

Fine sea salt

3 garlic cloves, finely chopped

3 parsley sprigs, chopped

Leaves from 1 thyme sprig (optional)

½ cup extra-virgin olive oil, divided

Freshly ground black pepper

1 medium yellow onion, thinly sliced

1 small green bell pepper, sliced

½ cup white wine

½ cup vegetable broth

1. Place the potatoes in a large bowl of cool water with 2 teaspoons salt. Let soak for at least 10 minutes.

2. Preheat the oven to 375°F.

3. Drain the potato slices, pat them dry, and place them in a large bowl. Add the garlic, parsley, thyme (if using), ¼ cup of the olive oil, and salt and pepper to taste. Mix until the potatoes are thoroughly coated.

4. Brush a 9-by-12-inch baking dish with the remaining ¼ cup olive oil. Place half of the potatoes in the dish and top with half of the onion and bell pepper. Add the remaining potatoes, followed by another layer of onion and bell pepper. Pour the wine and broth over the vegetables and season with ½ teaspoon black pepper. Cover the dish with aluminum foil.

5. Bake for 30 minutes. Remove the foil, raise the oven temperature to 410°F, and bake for another 30 minutes, until the potatoes are tender and a little crispy on the edges.

6. Serve on a platter. Store leftovers in an airtight container in the refrigerator for up to 3 days.

WINE PAIRING

The wine pairing will depend on the protein you serve the potatoes with. Have a godello or a rueda for fish and a tempranillo for beef or lamb.

Romesco Sauce

SALSA ROMESCO

Prep time: 15 minutes | Cook time: 40 minutes

This sauce originated in Valls, Tarragona, and dates back to 1896. It is typically eaten with Grilled Calçots (see page 41), a long, thin onion from Catalonia similar to a scallion. Romesco is also delicious with seafood, lamb, and poultry and is the perfect complement to a barbecue. Serve it with fish or escargot along with braised fennel and garnished with fresh mint. Sun-dried tomatoes are used here instead of the Spanish ñora (aka choricero) chile peppers, which are difficult to source in the United States. **MAKES 2 CUPS**

6 tomatoes on the vine

1 head garlic, unpeeled

1 cup extra-virgin olive oil, divided

4 marinated sun-dried tomatoes

2 slices toasted baguette

½ cup unsalted dry-roasted almonds, plus more if needed

½ cup unsalted dry-roasted hazelnuts, plus more if needed

1 tablespoon balsamic vinegar

1 teaspoon smoked paprika

Sea salt

Freshly ground black pepper

Red pepper flakes (optional)

1. Preheat the oven to 400°F.

2. Using a sharp knife, cut an "X" on the bottom of each tomato. Place the tomatoes and the whole head of garlic in a large baking pan and drizzle with 3 tablespoons of the olive oil.

3. Roast for 30 to 40 minutes, until the garlic head feels soft when pressed. Place the tomatoes in a bowl, cover with plastic wrap, and set aside to cool. Reserve the liquid from the pan. When cool, peel the tomatoes and remove the seeds; place the flesh in a food processor or blender and pour in the reserved liquid from the pan. When the garlic is cool enough to handle, squeeze the garlic cloves out of their skins into the food processor or blender.

4. Add the remaining ¾ cup plus 1 tablespoon olive oil, the sun-dried tomatoes, bread (if using), almonds, hazelnuts, vinegar, smoked paprika, salt and black pepper to taste, and a pinch of pepper flakes (if using). Process to a thick and creamy texture. If the mixture is too runny, blend in more almonds and hazelnuts. Store in an airtight container in the refrigerator for up to 3 days.

MAKE IT MORE TRADITIONAL

Swap in sherry vinegar for the balsamic. Or try both ways and see which you prefer. To make this with the traditional ñora peppers (which are dried), rehydrate 3 ñoras in a bowl of water for at least 4 hours, or up to overnight. Then remove the stems and seeds. Add the peppers in step 4 and omit the sun-dried tomatoes.

Mashed Potatoes with Paprika

PATATAS REVOLCONAS

Prep time: 15 minutes | Cook time: 30 minutes

A simple and tasty dish made with potatoes, smoked paprika, and crispy pork, *patatas revolconas* is a typical tapa at bars in Salamanca, Avila, and Extremadura, the lands of the famous Iberian pig. In Madrid's Chamberi neighborhood, there's a bar called Barrera that makes an exquisite version of this dish. It's especially good topped with fried eggs for brunch. **SERVES 4**

---

8 large Yukon Gold potatoes, peeled and each cut into 8 pieces

Splash white wine vinegar

1 teaspoon fine sea salt, plus more to taste

1 bay leaf

4 tablespoons extra-virgin olive oil, divided

8 ounces pancetta, diced

6 garlic cloves, minced

1 teaspoon smoked paprika

½ teaspoon cayenne pepper, or to taste

1 parsley sprig

1. In a large pot, combine the potatoes, water to cover, the vinegar, salt, and bay leaf. Bring to a boil over medium-high heat and cook for about 25 minutes, or until the potatoes are fork-tender. Remove the potatoes from the pot, reserving the water.

2. In a large sauté pan or skillet, heat 2 tablespoons of the olive oil over medium-high heat. When hot, add the pancetta and cook for about 5 minutes, until crispy on all sides, being careful not to burn it. Using a slotted spoon, transfer the pancetta to a plate.

3. Add the remaining 2 tablespoons olive oil to the pan. When hot, add the garlic and cook for about 2 minutes to lightly brown.

4. Remove the pan from the heat and stir in the paprika and cayenne. Add the potatoes to the pan little by little and begin to mash them with a potato masher or wooden spoon. If more moisture is needed to mash the potatoes, add some of the reserved water. Stir half of the pancetta into the mashed potatoes.

5. Serve the mashed potatoes in a large bowl, topped with the remaining pancetta and the parsley. Store leftovers in an airtight container in the refrigerator for up to 3 days.

DIFFERENT SPIN

The consistency of these mashed potatoes can vary, as some prefer a puree-like texture to a chunky texture. For a smoother texture, mash in more of the reserved water from boiling the potatoes. Some like to garnish this dish with crispy fried garlic slices.

BEVERAGE PAIRING

This dish pairs well with a cold amber ale. In Madrid there is a great amber ale made with toasted and caramelized malts called Jamonera from La Virgen brewery. If you prefer a glass of wine, pair it with a rosé of the garnacha varietal from Navarra, such as one from the Gran Feudo winery.

Spanish Ratatouille

PISTO MANCHEGO

Prep time: 15 minutes | Cook time: 45 minutes

You will find this adored traditional dish on the daily menu at neighborhood restaurants and bars. It can be served as a small first course or with fried eggs as an entrée. It makes a great brunch dish with fried eggs over roasted potatoes and some crispy prosciutto crumbled over the eggs.
SERVES 4

¼ cup extra-virgin olive oil

1 yellow onion, finely chopped

2 garlic cloves, minced

1 teaspoon fine sea salt

1 teaspoon fresh thyme leaves

1 medium red bell pepper, chopped

1 medium green bell pepper, chopped

2 small zucchini, diced

½ cup white wine

4 tomatoes on the vine, peeled (see Tip, page 51), seeded, and diced

1 teaspoon sherry vinegar or balsamic vinegar

1 teaspoon honey

1 parsley sprig, for garnish

1. In a large skillet, heat the olive oil over medium heat. When hot, add the onion, garlic, salt, and thyme and sauté for 15 minutes, until the onion turns translucent.

2. Add the bell peppers and sauté for about 10 minutes, until they soften. Add the zucchini and sauté for 3 minutes. Add the wine and simmer for 5 minutes.

3. Add the tomatoes, vinegar, and honey and simmer over low heat for about 20 minutes, until the mixture has a moist and tender consistency.

4. Serve garnished with the parsley. Store leftovers in an airtight container in the refrigerator for up to 3 days.

REGIONAL VARIATIONS

There are many regional renditions of this dish. In Andalucía, eggplant and potatoes are added. The *pisto* from Murcia has two beaten eggs and potatoes, but it does not have any red bell pepper or zucchini.

 WINE PAIRING

Pair this dish with a rosé of the garnacha or tempranillo varietal from Navarra.

Spanish Tomato Sauce

TOMATE FRITO

Prep time: 10 minutes | Cook time: 50 minutes

Every Spanish family takes pride in their own homemade tomato sauce, making it in large batches and freezing it. Having it ready ahead of time can be a lifesaver for a quick family dinner such as white rice, tomato sauce, and fried eggs; sautéed green beans with tomato sauce; or pasta with tomato sauce and chorizo. **MAKES 12 CUPS**

---

1 cup extra-virgin olive oil

3 yellow onions, thinly sliced

Sea salt

1 teaspoon sugar

½ cup water

Freshly ground
  black pepper

6 (28-ounce) cans
  tomato puree

1 bay leaf

½ cup red wine

1 tablespoon honey

1. In a large soup pot, heat the olive oil over medium heat. When hot, add the onions and sauté for 10 minutes, until soft. Sprinkle with salt to taste and the sugar and sauté for about 10 minutes more, until the onions begin to turn a light golden brown. Sauté for another 10 minutes, adding the water little by little, until the onions are golden brown. Season with salt and pepper.

2. Add the tomato puree, bay leaf, wine, and honey and simmer for 30 minutes, until the sauce starts to thicken. Season with salt and pepper to taste.

3. Let the sauce cool. Working in batches, transfer the sauce to a blender and blend to a thick and creamy texture. Store the sauce in an airtight container in the refrigerator for up to 5 days. Or divide the sauce into thirds, refrigerating one part to use right away (or within a few days) and freezing the other two portions in separate resealable freezer bags.

CHAPTER FOUR

Soups, Stews, and Cocidos

Soups, stews, and *cocidos* represent the backbone of Spanish regional cuisine. Every region has its specialties using local products. You may think that a *cocido* and a stew are the same, but they have one subtle difference. To stew means to cook all of the ingredients together in a pot. *Cocido* comes from the word *cocer*, which means "to cook," but everything is cooked separately in different pots and brought together at the end. Soups, enjoyed as a first course, are seasonal, which determines whether they are served hot or cold. Hot soups are served straight from the pot; cold soups are always garnished with ingredients that enhance their flavor.

Catalonian Fish Stew (page 73)

White Garlic Gazpacho

AJOBLANCO

Prep time: 20 minutes, plus 2 hours to chill

This dish is a popular cold soup from Granada, enjoyed during the hot summer months. It's wonderful garnished with cold peeled grapes: The contrast of the grapes' sweetness, the gazpacho's creamy texture, and the vinegar's acidity is magical. For a more sophisticated presentation, garnish your *ajoblanco* with a couple of cooked *gambas al ajillo* (Garlic Shrimp, page 15), or with tuna tartare. **SERVES 4**

1¼ cups slivered
   almonds, divided
2 garlic cloves,
   coarsely chopped
1 teaspoon fine sea salt

3½ cups cool water
½ cup cubed day-old
   round country bread
   (not sourdough),
   crusts removed

¼ cup sherry vinegar
½ cup extra-virgin olive oil
24 to 32 grapes, for garnish

1. In a blender, combine 1 cup of the almonds, the garlic, salt, and 1 cup of the water and blend to a coarse texture. Add the bread cubes, vinegar, and remaining 2½ cups water and blend until smooth. With the blender running, slowly add the olive oil. Blend until you achieve a creamy-looking texture.

2. Pour the soup through a fine-mesh sieve into a serving bowl to get a silky final texture.

3. Refrigerate to chill for up to 2 hours. This soup is best served cold.

4. Cut a tiny "X" on the bottom of each grape. Bring a medium pot of water to a boil, then add the grapes and blanch for about 40 seconds. Drain and transfer to a small bowl. Cover with plastic wrap and let cool for about 5 minutes. Peel each grape. Return them to the bowl and cover with plastic wrap. Refrigerate until the soup is ready to serve.

5. To serve, portion the soup into individual bowls and garnish with the remaining ¼ cup almonds and 6 to 8 peeled grapes. Store leftovers in an airtight container in the refrigerator for up to 1 day.

REGIONAL VARIATION

In Extremadura, this soup is made with egg yolk and does not contain almonds, but does include tomato and cucumber. In Malaga, it is garnished with moscatel grapes, melon, or apple.

 WINE PAIRING

Pair the white gazpacho with a fino or amontillado sherry. If you have a choice, the amontillado has a more complex structure and will work better with the garlic.

Andalucían Gazpacho

GAZPACHO ANDALUZ

Prep time: 15 minutes

Gazpacho is the emblematic cold tomato soup from Andalucía. It is a popular, humble, nutritious, and refreshing all-time favorite that is synonymous with summer. Gazpacho was originally made with tomatoes, day-old bread, garlic, peppers, and water, but this recipe omits the raw garlic and bread. Use your favorite olive oil here. **SERVES 4**

⅓ cup coarsely chopped red bell pepper

⅓ cup coarsely chopped green bell pepper

⅓ cup coarsely chopped sweet yellow onion

¼ cup coarsely chopped cucumber

2 pounds tomato on the vine, quartered

1 teaspoon sea salt

1½ teaspoon balsamic vinegar

½ cup extra-virgin olive oil

Optional toppings: chopped tomato, finely chopped sweet white onion, finely chopped red and green bell peppers, and chopped hard-boiled eggs

1. In a blender, combine the bell peppers, onion, cucumber, tomatoes, salt, vinegar, and olive oil. Blend on high speed for 10 to 15 minutes, until the gazpacho has an almost creamy texture. Spaniards like this soup very creamy and always strain it through a fine-mesh sieve after blending. If you prefer it slightly chunky, don't strain it.

2. Pour the gazpacho into bowls. If desired, top with any or all of the garnishes. Store leftovers in a pitcher covered with plastic wrap in the refrigerator for up to 2 days.

DIFFERENT SPIN

Instead of cucumber, add ½ cup chopped melon or seedless watermelon—a great choice during peak melon season. You can also use ½ cup finely chopped melon or watermelon as a topping.

 WINE PAIRING

Pair this soup with a fino sherry from the appellation of Jerez-Xérès-Sherry or with manzanilla sherry from Sanlúcar de Barrameda in Cádiz.

Galician Broth

CALDO GALLEGO

Prep time: 10 minutes | Cook time: 1 hour

This simple-to-make soup of Celtic origin is perfect to warm yourself on a typical windy and rainy day in Galicia. **SERVES 6**

2 ham hocks

1 slab pork ribs (12 ribs), cut into six 2-rib pieces

5 smoked bacon slices

1½ pounds Yukon Gold potatoes, peeled and sliced

2 (15.5-ounce) cans navy beans, drained and rinsed

3 cups chopped turnip greens

Sea salt

1. In a large soup pot, cover the ham hocks, ribs, and bacon with water. Bring to a boil over high heat, then reduce to a simmer, cover, and cook for 30 minutes. Check the broth as it simmers and use a skimmer or slotted spoon to remove any foam.

2. Gently stir in the potatoes, then return the soup to a boil and cook, uncovered, for another 20 minutes.

3. Stir in the beans and turnip greens, season with salt, and cook for another 10 to 15 minutes, until the greens are tender.

4. Remove the ham hock and ribs, cut the meat off the bones, and stir it into the soup. Discard the bones.

5. Serve in soup bowls or from a soup tureen. Store leftovers in an airtight container in the refrigerator for up to 5 days.

SUBSTITUTION

Kale, chard, or any dark leafy vegetable can be substituted for the turnip greens. Spinach is not recommended. Cannellini beans can be substituted for the navy beans.

 WINE PAIRING

Pair this soup with a Galician mencia from the Ribeira Sacra appellation.

Potato Leek Soup

PORRUSALDA

Prep time: 10 minutes | Cook time: 50 minutes

Porrusalda originated in the Basque Country and Navarra region, and it's perfect for a cold winter night. Its name means "leek broth" in Euskera (the Basque language). It is typically enjoyed during Lent. You can use vegetable broth, if you like. **SERVES 4**

¼ cup extra-virgin olive oil

1 yellow onion, finely chopped

Sea salt

3 (32-ounce) containers chicken broth

6 parsley sprigs

5 leeks, well rinsed and cut into ¾-inch pieces

2 large carrots, cut into ¾-inch pieces

3 large Yukon Gold potatoes, cut into ¾-inch-thick rounds

1. In a large soup pot, heat the olive oil over medium heat. When hot, add the onion and a pinch of salt and sauté for 10 minutes, until soft and translucent.

2. Add the broth and parsley. Bring to a boil over medium-high heat. Add the leeks, carrots, potatoes, and a pinch of salt. The liquid needs to cover all the vegetables, so add more broth or water if necessary. Mix well and boil for 25 to 30 minutes, until the potatoes are fork-tender.

3. To serve, pour the soup into individual bowls or a soup tureen. Store leftovers in an airtight container in the refrigerator for 3 to 4 days or freeze in a heavy-duty freezer bag.

MAKE IT MORE TRADITIONAL

Cut the potatoes into irregular shapes called *cachelos*. Start by sticking a knife about 1 inch into the potato, then break the piece off. By ripping the potato instead of slicing it, you create a greater surface area, releasing more starch into the dish to thicken the broth. This is a traditional Spanish cooking tip for stews and soups.

 WINE PAIRING

This soup will pair well with a rosé, preferably a tempranillo.

Tuna Pot

MARMITAKO DE ATÚN

Prep time: 10 minutes | Cook time: 50 minutes

The literal translation of *marmitako* is "what's in the pot?" It's a traditional and very popular Basque white tuna stew enjoyed aboard many fishing boats in the Cantabrian Sea. The dish is also called *marmita de bonito* (bonito pot) and *sorropotún* (a unique name for the dish) in Cantabria and Asturias, respectively. Although this delicious hot stew would be perfect for a cold winter night, it is customarily eaten in white tuna season, which is from June to September. **SERVES 4**

¼ cup extra-virgin olive oil

1 sweet yellow onion, finely chopped

2 garlic cloves, finely chopped

1 small green bell pepper, finely chopped

3 marinated sun-dried tomatoes, chopped (optional)

2 tomatoes on the vine, grated on a box grater

½ teaspoon red pepper flakes

1½ teaspoons smoked paprika

1 teaspoon fine sea salt

¾ cup dry white wine

Flaky sea salt

3 medium russet potatoes, peeled and cubed

2 quarts fish stock or vegetable broth, hot

12 ounces white tuna, red tuna, or any firm white-fleshed fish, cut into 1-inch cubes

Freshly ground black pepper

Leaves from 3 parsley sprigs, for garnish

1. In a large soup pot, heat the olive oil over medium heat. When hot, add the onion, garlic, and bell pepper and sauté for 15 minutes, or until the onion is soft and translucent.

2. Stir in the sun-dried tomatoes (if using) and grated tomato and cook for 3 minutes to release the tomato liquid. Stir in the pepper flakes, smoked paprika, salt, and wine. Cook for 2 to 3 minutes to meld the flavors.

3. Stir in the potatoes and pour in the hot stock. Bring to a boil, then reduce the heat to low and simmer for 25 minutes, or until the potatoes are fork-tender.

CONTINUED

4. Stir in the tuna, cover, and remove from the heat. Let stand for 5 minutes. Season with salt and pepper.

5. Serve the soup in bowls, garnished with the parsley leaves. Store leftovers in an airtight container in the refrigerator for up to 3 days.

MAKE IT MORE TRADITIONAL

If you can find dried Spanish choricero pepper, use it in place of the sun-dried tomatoes here. You'll need ¾ ounce, and it needs to be rehydrated first.

TECHNIQUE TIP

To thicken the sauce, rather than smoothly slicing the potatoes, it is typical in Spanish cooking to break chunks off by inserting a knife and breaking off small irregular pieces. These are called *cachelos*. This method provides more surface area and thus releases more starch, which will give you a nice thick broth.

 WINE PAIRING

Pair this dish with a godello white wine from Valdeorras, Galicia, with tropical fruit, mineral, and floral notes.

Potato Chicken Stew

PATATAS CON POLLO

Prep time: 15 minutes | Cook time: 1 hour

Patatas con pollo is a sumptuous stew that should be enjoyed with wonderful company, great wine, and lots of laughter. **SERVES 6**

1½ pounds boneless, skinless chicken thighs, cut into 2-inch pieces

1 tablespoon fresh thyme

Sea salt

Freshly ground black pepper

10 tablespoons extra-virgin olive oil, divided

4 garlic cloves, minced, divided

1 medium yellow onion, chopped

1 green bell pepper, chopped

1 red bell pepper, chopped

1 tomato on the vine, grated on a box grater

4 russet potatoes, peeled and cut into cachelos (see Tip, page 68)

½ teaspoon saffron threads

4 rosemary sprigs

4 quarts chicken broth, hot

⅓ cup Arborio rice

Red pepper flakes

8 ounces mushrooms, sliced

1. Sprinkle the chicken with the thyme and season with salt and black pepper.

2. In a large pot, heat 5 tablespoons of the olive oil over medium heat. When hot, add the chicken and cook for 15 minutes, or until browned on all sides. Remove the chicken and set aside.

3. Reduce the heat under the pot to medium and add 3 tablespoons of the olive oil. When hot, add two-thirds of the garlic and sauté for 2 minutes, or until browned. Add the onion and season with salt and black pepper. Sauté for about 15 minutes, until the onion is soft and translucent.

4. Add the bell peppers and a pinch of salt. Sauté for 5 minutes, or until the peppers are tender. Add the grated tomato and cook for 2 minutes to release the liquid.

5. Add the potatoes, mixing well to release their starch. Add the browned chicken, saffron, rosemary, and hot broth. The liquid should cover all the ingredients, so add more broth or water if necessary. Bring to a boil over high heat, then reduce the heat to medium and cook, uncovered, for 10 minutes.

6. Stir in the rice and cook, uncovered, for 20 minutes, until the potatoes are tender and the rice is cooked.

CONTINUED

7. Meanwhile, in a medium skillet, heat the remaining 2 tablespoons olive oil over medium-high heat. Add the remaining garlic and season with pepper flakes to taste. Sauté for about 2 minutes, until the garlic is lightly browned. Add the mushrooms and sauté for about 5 minutes, until they soften. Season with salt.

8. Stir the mushroom mixture into the stew.

9. Serve the stew in bowls or pasta dishes. Store leftovers in an airtight container in the refrigerator for up to 3 to 4 days or freeze in an airtight container or freezer bag for up to 3 months.

MAKE IT MORE TRADITIONAL

Traditionally this dish is made with rabbit and is called *patatas con conejo*. To prepare it with rabbit, skip steps 1 and 2 and omit the 5 tablespoons olive oil. Cut the rabbit into pieces, place it in a soup pot, and add water to cover. Add the thyme and boil for 30 minutes. In step 5, add the rabbit and its cooking liquid (omit the chicken broth) and proceed with the recipe. Also, use Spanish bomba rice instead of Arborio.

 WINE PAIRING

Red wines of the tempranillo and garnacha varietals will pair well with this stew.

Chickpea, Butternut Squash, and Green Bean Stew

POTAJE DE GARBANZOS, CALABAZA, Y JUDÍAS VERDES

Prep time: 15 minutes | Cook time: 40 minutes

This traditional stew from Chiclana is a great vegetarian *cocido* option. In this version, ready-to-eat marinated sun-dried tomatoes stand in for *pimientos choriceros*, Spanish chiles that are difficult to find in the United States. **SERVES 4**

FOR THE STEW

½ cup extra-virgin olive oil

1 medium yellow onion, finely chopped

1 leek, white and light green parts only, well rinsed and finely chopped

2 garlic cloves, minced or pressed in a garlic press

1 teaspoon fine sea salt, plus more for seasoning

5 large Yukon Gold potatoes, peeled and cut into large chunks

8 ounces green beans, trimmed and cut into thirds

2 teaspoons fresh thyme

Freshly ground black pepper

4 marinated sun-dried tomatoes, chopped

1 tomato on the vine, grated on a box grater

Red pepper flakes (optional)

6 saffron threads

½ cup white wine

1 butternut squash, peeled, seeded, and cut into 1-inch cubes

7 cups vegetable broth

1 bay leaf

2 (16.5-ounce) cans chickpeas, drained and rinsed

FOR THE GARNISH

4 tomatoes on the vine, halved

Fine sea salt

2 garlic cloves, minced or pressed in a garlic press

5 teaspoons extra-virgin olive oil

1 bunch mint, sprigs separated

TO MAKE THE STEW

1. In a large soup pot, heat the olive oil over medium-low heat. When hot, add the onion, leek, garlic, and salt and cook, stirring occasionally, for about 10 minutes, until the onion and leek are softened and translucent.

CONTINUED

2. Add the potatoes and green beans and cook for a few minutes. Stir in the thyme, black pepper, sun-dried tomatoes, grated tomato, and pepper flakes (if using). Stir in the saffron, mixing well, then the wine. Cook for 2 minutes to burn off the alcohol.

3. Stir in the squash and broth. Bring to a boil over high heat, add the bay leaf, and gently mix in the chickpeas. Reduce the heat to low and simmer for 25 minutes, until the squash and potatoes are tender. Taste and adjust the seasonings.

TO MAKE THE GARNISH

4. Use the large holes of a box grater to grate the tomatoes into a bowl. Season to taste with salt, add the garlic, and mix well. Add the olive oil and mix well with a fork or whisk.

5. Serve the stew in soup or pasta bowls, garnished with a sprig of fresh mint and accompanied by a bowl of the tomato-garlic garnish. Store leftovers in an airtight container in the refrigerator for 3 to 4 days or in the freezer for up to 3 months.

 WINE PAIRING

An oak-aged chardonnay will pair well with this stew; if you prefer a red, have a tempranillo from Ribera del Duero.

Catalonian Fish Stew

SUQUET DE PESCADO

Prep time: 15 minutes | Cook time: 30 minutes

Suquet is the Catalonian word for the pot used to make this dish. Like the *marmitako de atún* (Tuna Pot, page 67), it started out as a humble dish created by fishermen with leftover fish scraps. It has now evolved to "haute cuisine" and can be made with any kind of fish or shellfish. To thicken the sauce, take some of the potatoes out, mash them, then mix them back in. Omit the cornstarch if you do this. **SERVES 4**

5 tablespoons extra-virgin olive oil

4 garlic cloves, minced

4 tablespoons finely chopped fresh parsley, divided

5 tablespoons grated tomato

2 teaspoons smoked paprika

1½ pounds russet potatoes, peeled and cut into 1-inch cubes

2½ cups fish stock

2 pounds mahimahi, cut into 2-inch pieces

Sea salt

Freshly ground black pepper

1 tablespoon cornstarch, dissolved in 1 tablespoon cold water

Aioli (page 40), for serving

1. In a large sauté pan or skillet, heat the olive oil over medium-high heat. When hot, add the garlic and cook for about 1 minute to lightly brown. When it begins to brown, stir in 2 tablespoons of the parsley and the grated tomato. Reduce the heat to medium and cook for 5 minutes to reduce the liquid from the tomato.

2. Stir in the paprika, potatoes, and 1¼ cups of the fish stock. Bring to a boil over medium-high heat, then reduce to a simmer and cook, uncovered, for 20 minutes, until the potatoes are tender. Add the remaining 1¼ cups fish stock little by little as the liquid in the pan reduces.

3. Season the mahimahi with salt and pepper, add it to the pan, and cook for 3 minutes. Taste and season with salt and pepper if needed. Add the cornstarch mixture, stirring carefully so that you don't break up the fish or potatoes. Cook for 5 minutes to thicken the stew and finish cooking the fish.

CONTINUED

4. Serve the stew in bowls or pasta dishes, garnished with the remaining 2 tablespoons parsley, with a bowl of aioli on the side. Store leftovers in an airtight container in the refrigerator for up to 3 days.

MAKE IT MORE TRADITIONAL

In addition to the aioli, this stew can be served with a *picada*—a mélange of ingredients that will enhance the dish's flavors. In a blender, combine 2 garlic cloves, 1 teaspoon slivered almonds, 1 teaspoon pine nuts, 1 slice fried French bread, 2 sprigs parsley, 6 saffron threads, and 1 tablespoon extra-virgin olive oil and pulse until you achieve a coarse grainy texture.

Madrid-Style Chickpea Stew

COCIDO MADRILEÑO

Prep time: 10 minutes | Cook time: 1 hour

A cold and rainy Saturday can become perfect with a *cocido madrileño* to enjoy with friends and family, accompanied by a good bottle of wine. It is served in three stages (or *vuelcos*, which means "turning of the pots"): first a brothy soup with noodles; then the platter of stewed meats; and finally the veggies. **SERVES 6**

FOR THE STEW

8 ounces beef stew meat

1 ham shank

1 ham hock

4 ounces smoked bacon

1 link chorizo

2 boneless, skinless chicken thighs, cut into thirds

2 cups canned chickpeas, drained and rinsed

2 carrots, cut into thirds

3 large Yukon Gold potatoes, peeled and cut into thirds

½ yellow onion

¼ head green cabbage

Fine sea salt

½ cup extra-virgin olive oil

2 garlic cloves, sliced

2 cups fideo noodles or broken angel hair pasta

FOR SERVING

4 tomatoes on the vine, halved

Fine sea salt

Pinch ground cumin

2 garlic cloves, minced or pressed in a garlic press

Leaves from 1 mint sprig, chopped

5 teaspoons extra-virgin olive oil

TO MAKE THE STEW

1. In a large soup pot, combine the beef, ham shank, ham hock, bacon, chorizo, chicken, and cold water to cover. Bring to a boil over high heat, then reduce the heat to medium. Over the next 10 minutes, use a skimmer or slotted spoon to remove any foam that surfaces. Reduce the heat to a simmer, cover, and cook for at least 30 minutes, preferably 45 minutes. The longer the broth simmers, the more flavor it will have. After 25 minutes, add the chickpeas.

2. Meanwhile, in a separate large pot, combine the carrots, potatoes, onion, cabbage, and cold water to cover. Add 1 teaspoon salt and bring to a boil over high heat. Reduce the heat to medium and cook, uncovered, for 25 to 30 minutes, until the potatoes are fork-tender.

CONTINUED

3. Scoop the potatoes, carrots, and onion out of the broth onto a platter. Cover with aluminum foil to keep warm. Pour the broth and cabbage into a sieve set over a bowl. Place the cabbage in a separate bowl and transfer the broth to a medium pot.

4. In a medium sauté pan or skillet, heat the olive oil over medium heat. When hot, add the garlic and sauté for 2 minutes to lightly brown. Pour the garlic and oil over the cabbage, season with salt, and mix well. Cover with foil to keep warm.

5. Preheat the oven to 250°F.

6. Scoop the meat, chorizo, chicken, and chickpeas onto a large ovenproof platter or baking dish. Cut the meat off the ham shank and hock and add it to the platter (discard the bones). Cover with foil and keep warm in the oven.

7. Strain the meat broth through a fine-mesh sieve to remove any solids. Add this broth to the vegetable broth in the pot. Taste and season with salt if needed.

8. To make the soup, add the noodles to the pot of broth and bring to a boil over medium-high heat. Cook for 5 to 8 minutes, until the noodles are cooked through.

TO SERVE

9. Use the large holes of a box grater to grate the tomatoes into a bowl. Season to taste with salt, add the cumin, garlic, and mint, and mix well. Add the olive oil and mix well with a fork or a whisk.

10. Serve the brothy noodles in soup bowls as a first course. Follow with the platter of meats and chickpeas served family-style. Accompany with the tomato mixture. Separately, serve the platter of vegetables and bowl of cabbage. Store leftovers in an airtight container in the refrigerator for 3 to 4 days or freeze in an airtight container or freezer bag for up to 3 months.

MAKE IT MORE TRADITIONAL

For a more authentic taste, seek out Palacios brand chorizo online. It comes in spicy or regular.

 WINE PAIRING

A red wine of the monastrell varietal from the appellation of Jumilla or a mencia from Bierzo will pair nicely with this *cocido*.

Tolosa-Style Beans with Trimmings

ALUBIAS DE TOLOSA CON SUS SACRAMENTOS

Prep time: 10 minutes | Cook time: 45 minutes

This succulent bean dish with pickled peppers, crispy ribs, and pork belly is even better if you seek out Palacios brand Spanish chorizo, either spicy or regular. **SERVES 4**

---

8 pork ribs, separated

4 ounces pork belly, cut into 1-inch cubes

8 ounces chorizo, cut into 6 pieces

½ cup white wine

Sea salt

½ cup plus 2 tablespoons extra-virgin olive oil, divided

1 small yellow onion, finely chopped

1 leek, white and light green parts only, well rinsed and finely chopped

1 small green bell pepper, diced

3 (15.5-ounce) cans kidney beans, drained and rinsed

½ head green cabbage, thinly sliced

2 garlic cloves, finely chopped

⅓ cup beef broth or vegetable broth

16 pepperoncini

1. In a large soup pot, combine the ribs, pork belly, chorizo, and cold water to cover. Add the wine and a pinch of salt and bring to a boil over high heat. Reduce the heat to medium-low, cover, and simmer for 30 minutes to render out some of the fat. Place the ribs, pork belly, and chorizo on a platter and set aside. (Discard the cooking water.)

2. In a medium sauté pan or skillet, heat ¼ cup of the olive oil over low heat. When hot, add the onion, leek, and a pinch of salt and sauté for about 15 minutes, until soft and translucent. Add the bell pepper and sauté until soft, about 10 minutes.

3. Add the kidney beans and just enough water to cover them. Bring to a boil, then reduce the heat to a simmer and cook for 20 to 25 minutes, until a creamy texture is obtained. As the liquid in the pan reduces, add water as needed to keep the beans just covered.

4. Bring a small pot of water to a boil with a pinch of salt. Add the cabbage and boil for 10 minutes. Drain and transfer to a bowl or plate.

CONTINUED

5. In a medium sauté pan or skillet, heat ¼ cup of the olive oil over medium heat. When hot, add the garlic and sauté for 1 minute to lightly brown. Pour the garlic and oil over the cabbage in the bowl.

6. Line a plate with paper towels. In a large skillet, heat the remaining 2 tablespoons olive oil over medium-high heat. When hot, add the ribs and pork belly and cook for 3 minutes. When the pork begins to crisp, add the broth and cook for 2 to 4 minutes more, until crispy. Transfer to the paper towel–lined plate to drain.

7. Serve the kidney beans in bowls or pasta dishes garnished with the pepperoncini. Serve the meats on a platter and the garlic-seasoned cabbage family-style in a separate bowl for everyone to help themselves at the table. Store leftovers in an airtight container in the refrigerator for up to 3 days.

MAKE IT MORE TRADITIONAL

For a more authentic preparation, start with dried kidney beans. Soak them in cold water overnight and cook the beans for about 2 hours in step 3 following the same instructions. The texture of the cooked beans should be creamy.

 WINE PAIRING
Pair this dish with a tempranillo from La Rioja or Ribera del Duero.

CHAPTER FIVE

Rice and Pasta

A Sunday family gathering in Spain without paella is unimaginable. The country's rice dishes originated in Valencia, famous for its marshes filled with rice fields and the fresh produce from its gardens. This chapter will teach you the three techniques used in cooking Spanish-style rice dishes: paella-style rice, honeyed rice, and brothy rice, along with an endless list of combinable ingredients. But rice is not the only carb that Spaniards enjoy. Another favorite is pasta, used in the array of noodle dishes found throughout Spain. In this chapter, you will also discover that the key ingredient for both rice and noodle dishes is the broth.

Mixed Paella (page 82)

Mixed Paella

PAELLA MIXTA

Prep time: 15 minutes | Cook time: 45 minutes

Paella mixta is the queen of all paellas. This dish can be found on every Spanish beach-restaurant menu. Its name comes from the combination of pork, chicken, seafood, and veggies it contains. A large paella pan is helpful for cooking and spreading out the ingredients (traditionally over an evenly distributed fire), but it's not necessary. It can also be done in a skillet on your stovetop and finished off in the oven. You can use just one type of broth or a mixture. **SERVES 4**

2¼ cups chicken broth

2 cups fish stock

Sea salt

Freshly ground
   black pepper

8 mussels

½ cup white wine

5 tablespoons extra-virgin
   olive oil, divided

6 to 8 shrimp, unpeeled

½ cup finely chopped
   yellow onion

2 garlic cloves,
   finely chopped

½ red bell pepper, chopped

2 boneless, skinless
   chicken thighs, cut into
   1-inch pieces

4 ounces chorizo, diced

4 ounces green beans,
   trimmed and cut into
   1-inch pieces

1 marinated sun-dried
   tomato, chopped
   (optional)

4 tomatoes on the vine,
   grated on a box grater

1 teaspoon smoked paprika

½ teaspoon saffron threads

2 cups Arborio rice

1 lemon, cut into wedges

1 parsley sprig

1. Preheat the oven to 375°F.

2. In a large soup pot, combine the chicken broth and fish stock over medium heat to slowly heat up the broth. Keep the broth hot. Season well with salt and pepper.

3. In a large sauté pan or skillet, combine the mussels and wine. Cover the pan, set over medium-high heat, and steam the mussels for 3 to 5 minutes, until they open. Discard any unopened mussels. Transfer the mussels to a plate and set aside. Pour the liquid from the pan into the pot with the broth.

4. In a large ovenproof skillet, preferably cast iron, heat 2 tablespoons of the olive oil over medium-high heat. When hot, add the shrimp and sauté for 3 to 4 minutes, just until they turn pink. Remove the shrimp to a plate and set aside to cool, then peel them and add the shells to the broth.

5. In the same skillet, heat the remaining 3 tablespoons olive oil over low heat. When hot, add the onion and garlic and sauté for 15 minutes, until translucent.

6. Add the bell pepper and sauté for 10 minutes, or until soft. Add the chicken, season with salt and black pepper, and sauté for 10 to 15 minutes, until browned. Add the chorizo and cook for about 5 minutes.

7. Stir in the green beans and the sun-dried tomato (if using), mixing well. Stir in the grated tomato and cook until it releases its liquid, about 2 minutes. Stir in the smoked paprika and saffron. Add the rice and toast it, stirring frequently, for 5 minutes.

8. Strain the broth through a fine-mesh sieve; it should measure 4¼ cups (add water if necessary to get to this amount). Add it to the skillet. Increase the heat to high and cook for 5 minutes.

9. Transfer the skillet to the oven to finish cooking, about 15 minutes.

10. Remove the skillet from the oven and garnish the paella with the shrimp and mussels. Cover the skillet with a clean kitchen towel and let stand for 5 minutes.

11. Serve garnished with the lemon wedges and a parsley sprig. Leftovers can be stored in an airtight container in the refrigerator for up to 4 days.

MAKE IT MORE TRADITIONAL
Use bomba rice and pimentón de la Vera (Spanish smoked paprika).

 WINE PAIRING
Pair your paella with Sangria (page 139), a rosé from Navarra, or a verdejo from Rueda.

Seafood Rice

ARROZ A BANDA

Prep time: 10 minutes | Cook time: 40 minutes

Though most Spaniards don't eat the seafood that is used to make the stock for this dish (because the full flavor of it is in the rice already), in this rendition it gets served along with the rice. But if you'd prefer, save the leftover seafood to use in place of the ham in *croquetas de jamón* (Cured Ham Croquettes, page 18). Just chop it up and add it to the béchamel instead of the ham. **SERVES 4**

FOR THE SEAFOOD STOCK

2 leeks, well rinsed, each cut into 4 pieces

1 yellow onion, coarsely chopped

8 parsley sprigs

1 bay leaf, torn in half

1 small whole sea bass or branzino, cleaned and cut into quarters

8 ounces halibut, cut into 3 fillets

1 whole crab, cut in half

20 shell-on prawns, halved lengthwise

3 lobster tails (optional)

Sea salt

Freshly ground black pepper

FOR THE PAELLA

3 tablespoons extra-virgin olive oil

2 garlic cloves, finely chopped

½ teaspoon saffron threads

¼ cup Spanish Tomato Sauce (page 59) or store-bought

2½ cups Arborio rice

1 lemon, halved

2 parsley sprigs

Aioli (page 40), for serving

TO MAKE THE SEAFOOD STOCK

1. In a large soup pot, combine the leeks, onion, parsley, bay leaf, sea bass, halibut, crab, prawns, lobster tails (if using), and enough water to cover all of the ingredients. Bring to a boil over high heat, then reduce the heat to medium and cook for 15 to 20 minutes. This will make a flavorful but not overpowering fish stock. During cooking, skim off and discard the foam that forms on the surface.

2. Strain the fish stock through a fine-mesh sieve. Return the strained stock to the pot and place it over low heat to keep hot. Season it well with salt and pepper. Set the fish, crab, prawns, and lobster aside.

3. Preheat the oven to 375°F.

4. In a large cast-iron or other ovenproof skillet, heat the olive oil over medium heat. When hot, add the garlic and sauté for 2 minutes. Stir the saffron into the garlic, then quickly add the tomato sauce and mix well. Stir in the rice and cook, stirring frequently, for about 5 minutes, until it turns opaque.

5. Add 5½ cups of the hot stock and mix well. Increase the heat to bring the liquid to a boil and cook for 5 minutes.

6. Place the skillet in the oven for 15 minutes to finish cooking.

7. Remove the skillet from the oven, cover it with a clean kitchen towel, and let sit for 5 to 10 minutes.

8. Serve the paella out of the skillet, garnished with the lemon halves and parsley sprigs, with a bowl of aioli alongside. Place the reserved fish, shrimp, crab, and lobster on a plate or platter and serve with the rice and aioli. The rice can be stored in an airtight container in the refrigerator for up to 3 days. The seafood can be stored in a separate airtight container in the refrigerator for up to 3 days.

MAKE IT MORE TRADITIONAL

Spaniards also like to accompany rice dishes like this with sliced peeled tomatoes seasoned with flaky sea salt and extra-virgin olive oil. Also, to be more authentic, use bomba rice in place of Arborio.

 WINE PAIRING

A light and fruity albariño from Galicia will pair nicely with the seafood flavors of this rice dish.

Squid Ink Black Rice

ARROZ NEGRO

Prep time: 10 minutes | Cook time: 50 minutes

Arroz negro is for the adventurous who are willing to try squid ink. The ink turns the rice black, and its rich, briny flavor will captivate you and have you craving this wonderful Spanish dish over and over. To get the most explosive combination of flavors, pair this with Aioli (page 40), its inseparable companion in Spain. **SERVES 4**

FOR THE BROTH

4½ cups fish stock

4 ounces squid

½ cup white wine

4 (4-gram) pouches
   squid ink

Sea salt

FOR THE RICE

5 tablespoons extra-virgin
   olive oil

2 small yellow onions,
   finely chopped

4 garlic cloves,
   finely chopped

Sea salt

Freshly ground
   black pepper

4 tomatoes on the vine,
   grated on a box grater

1 pound calamari
   steaks, diced

2 cups bomba or
   Arborio rice

1 lemon, halved

1 parsley sprig

TO MAKE THE BROTH

1. In a medium soup pot, combine the stock and squid and bring to a boil over medium-high heat, then reduce to a simmer and cook for 20 minutes.

2. In a small bowl, whisk together the wine and squid ink. Stir this into the pot with the stock. Season well with salt.

3. Strain the hot broth through a fine-mesh sieve. Return it to the pot and keep hot over low heat.

TO MAKE THE RICE

4. Preheat the oven to 375°F.

5. In a large cast-iron or other ovenproof skillet, heat the olive oil over low heat. When hot, add the onions and garlic and season with salt and pepper. Cook, stirring occasionally, for 20 to 25 minutes, until the onions are lightly golden. Add the grated tomatoes and stir for 2 minutes to release their liquid.

6. Increase the heat to medium and stir in the diced squid. Cook, stirring occasionally, for 10 minutes. Stir in the rice and toast it, stirring frequently, for 5 minutes, or until it turns opaque. Measure the strained hot broth; you should have 4¼ cups (add water if necessary to get to this amount). Add the broth to the pan, bring to a boil over high heat, and cook for 5 minutes.

7. Transfer the skillet to the oven and cook for 15 minutes.

8. Remove the skillet from the oven, cover it with a clean kitchen towel, and let sit for 5 minutes.

9. Serve the rice from the skillet, garnished with the lemon halves and parsley sprig. Store leftovers in an airtight container in the refrigerator for up to 3 days.

REGIONAL VARIATION

Some preparations include shrimp and mussels. Peel the uncooked shrimp and add the shells to the fish stock to enhance the flavor of the broth. Sauté the shrimp in extra-virgin olive oil until they turn pink and add them to the skillet before you place it in the oven. Meanwhile, for the mussels, steam them in ½ cup white wine. When you remove the rice from the oven, place the mussels on top of the rice before you cover it with the towel.

 WINE PAIRING

A red wine from Empordà, Catalonia: Cabernet sauvignon, merlot, cariñena, and garnacha varietals will pair nicely with *arroz negro*.

"Honeyed" Shrimp Rice

ARROZ MELOSO DE GAMBAS

Prep time: 10 minutes | Cook time: 50 minutes

There are three ways to prepare rice in Spain: brothy, paella-style, or "honeyed." "Honeyed" refers to the texture, not an ingredient. *Arroz meloso* can be made with whatever you have at hand: vegetables, meat, fish. The three key factors are the starchy rice for a creamy, sticky texture; the broth; and the sofrito, which is the mixture of sautéed onions, peppers, garlic, and leeks—a must to start any Spanish rice dish. **SERVES 4**

5 tablespoons extra-virgin olive oil, divided

16 large shrimp, unpeeled

6 cups fish stock

1 cup dry white wine

1 leek, white and light green parts only, well rinsed and finely chopped

1 sweet yellow onion, finely chopped

1 garlic clove, finely chopped

1 red bell pepper, finely chopped

1 green bell pepper, finely chopped

2 tomatoes on the vine, grated on a box grater

1 teaspoon smoked paprika

½ teaspoon saffron threads

Sea salt

2 cups bomba or Arborio rice

2 parsley sprigs, finely chopped

1. In a nonstick medium sauté pan or skillet, heat 2 tablespoons of the olive oil over medium-high heat. When hot, add the shrimp and sauté for 3 minutes, until half cooked through and pink. Transfer to a plate until cool enough to handle, then peel the shrimp and reserve the shells. Set the shrimp aside.

2. In a large pot, combine the stock, wine, and reserved shrimp shells and bring to a boil over high heat. Reduce the heat to a simmer to keep the stock hot.

3. In the same sauté pan or skillet, heat the remaining 3 tablespoons olive oil over medium heat. When hot, add the leek, onion, and garlic and sauté for 15 minutes, until soft and translucent. Add the bell peppers and sauté for 7 minutes, or until tender. Add the grated tomatoes and sauté for 5 minutes to release their liquid.

4. Add the smoked paprika and saffron to the fish stock. Season well with salt.

5. Add the rice to the pan with the vegetables and toast, stirring frequently, for 5 minutes.

6. Strain the stock (discard the shrimp shells). Add 1 cup of stock to the rice mixture and cook, stirring occasionally, until the liquid has been almost completely absorbed. Add another cup of stock and continue cooking, stirring occasionally, and adding more stock as it is absorbed by the rice. Gradually adding the stock to the rice little by little gives it the "honeyed" texture. Cook, stirring occasionally, for 17 to 20 minutes, until the rice is cooked through but still a bit al dente.

7. Stir in the shrimp and cook for 2 minutes longer. Remove from the heat, cover the pan with a clean kitchen towel, and let sit for 15 minutes.

8. Serve in a bowl topped with the parsley. Store any leftovers in an airtight container in the refrigerator for up to 4 days.

TECHNIQUE TIP

To use a box grater to grate tomatoes the way the Spaniards do, first cut a tiny bit off of the tomato's bottom to give you a flat surface to start with. Then grate the tomato on the large holes of the grater into a bowl (to collect the flesh and juices), leaving the skin behind. (Grated tomato is really the best option, but in a pinch you can substitute canned tomatoes.)

 WINE PAIRING

A white wine like a fruity, minerally godello from the Valdeorras appellation or a light-bodied herbaceous verdejo from Rueda will pair nicely with your "honeyed" rice.

Vegetable Garden Rice

ARROZ DE LA HUERTA

Prep time: 15 minutes | Cook time: 40 minutes

This dish is also known as *arroz viudo* ("widowed rice") because it doesn't have meat or fish. It uses any vegetables you might have on hand, so be ingenious and creative. Spaniards enjoy a touch of cured ham with their veggies, so add some chopped prosciutto if you want. **SERVES 4**

FOR THE BROTH

4½ cups vegetable broth

2 parsley sprigs

1 leek, cleaned and cut into 4 pieces

½ white onion

Sea salt

Freshly ground black pepper

FOR THE RICE

3 tablespoons extra-virgin olive oil

½ yellow onion, finely chopped

2 garlic cloves, finely chopped

½ cup chopped red bell pepper

3 medium artichokes

1 lemon, halved

½ cup asparagus tips

4 ounces chopped prosciutto (optional)

1 marinated sun-dried tomato (optional) chopped

4 ounces green beans, trimmed and cut into thirds

3 tomatoes on the vine, grated on a box grater

1 teaspoon smoked paprika

½ teaspoon saffron threads

½ cup frozen shelled edamame, thawed

½ cup green peas

2 cups bomba or Arborio rice

TO MAKE THE BROTH

1. In a medium soup pot, combine the broth, parsley, leek, and onion. Season well with salt and pepper. Heat over medium-high heat until hot, then reduce the heat to low and keep the broth hot until needed.

TO MAKE THE RICE

2. Preheat the oven to 375°F.

3. In a large cast-iron or other ovenproof skillet, heat the olive oil over low heat. When hot, add the onion and garlic and sauté for 15 minutes, until translucent. Add the bell pepper and sauté for 10 minutes, until soft.

4. Meanwhile, clean the artichokes by cutting off the stems and removing the outer darker green leaves until you get to the lighter-colored inner leaves. Cut one-third off of the top and carefully cut around the bottom where the stem was, leaving it nice and clean. Use a spoon to scrape out the fuzzy choke from the middle. Rub the artichoke with the lemon, then thinly slice lengthwise.

5. Stir the artichoke slices and asparagus tips into the skillet and sauté for 5 minutes.

6. If using the prosciutto and sun-dried tomato, add them and sauté for 4 minutes. Add the green beans and sauté for 5 minutes. Stir in the grated tomatoes and cook for 2 minutes to release their liquid. Stir in the smoked paprika, saffron, edamame, and peas and mix well.

7. Add the rice and toast well, stirring frequently, for 5 minutes. Measure out 4½ cups of the hot broth (add water if necessary to come to that amount). Add the broth to the pan, increase the heat to high, and cook for 5 minutes. Transfer the skillet to the oven for 15 minutes to finish cooking.

8. Remove the skillet from the oven, cover it with a clean kitchen towel, and let sit for 15 minutes.

9. Serve the rice directly from the skillet. Store any leftovers in an airtight container in the refrigerator for up to 5 days.

 WINE PAIRING
A nice dry verdejo from Rueda will pair nicely with this rice dish.

Sailor's Rice

ARROZ MARINERO

Prep time: 15 minutes | Cook time: 55 minutes

Arroz marinero is a brothy seafood lover's favorite. It's the perfect dish to entertain on a chilly spring day. Feel free to use your preferred fish or shellfish, as the dish is intended to be chock-full of treasures from the sea. A large wok is perfect for cooking this dish if you have one. Freeze any leftover fish stock for future recipes or to fortify any stock needed for some of the other rice and noodle dishes in this book. **SERVES 4**

4 tablespoons extra-virgin olive oil, divided

1 pound shrimp, unpeeled

10 cups fish stock

Sea salt

Freshly ground black pepper

12 clams, such as manila

1 cup white wine

2 small yellow onions, finely chopped

1 large garlic clove, finely chopped

1 teaspoon smoked paprika

½ teaspoon saffron threads

2 tomatoes on the vine, grated on a box grater

8 ounces squid rings

2 cups bomba or Arborio rice

4 mint sprigs

1. In large deep pot or wok, heat 1 tablespoon of the olive oil over medium-high heat. When hot, add the shrimp and sauté for 2 minutes, or until pink in color. Remove the shrimp and set aside. When cool enough to handle, peel the shrimp and reserve the shells.

2. In a medium soup pot, combine the fish stock and reserved shrimp shells and set over high heat. When the stock is hot, reduce the heat to a simmer to keep warm. Season with salt and pepper.

3. In a small skillet, combine the clams and wine. Set over medium-high heat, cover, and steam for 3 to 5 minutes, until the clams open. Discard any unopened clams. Place the clams on a plate and set aside. Add the steaming liquid to the pot with the stock and season with more salt and pepper if needed.

4. In the same pot or wok used to cook the shrimp, heat the remaining 3 tablespoons olive oil over low heat. When hot, add the onions and garlic and sauté for 15 minutes, until soft and translucent. Stir in the smoked paprika and the saffron, then quickly add the grated tomatoes and sauté for 2 more minutes to release their liquid. Add the squid rings and sauté for 2 minutes.

5. Strain the hot stock through a fine-mesh sieve. Pour 6 cups of the stock into the pot. Increase the heat to high and bring to a boil. Keep remaining stock hot in a separate pot on a separate burner.

6. Stir in rice and cook over high heat for 5 minutes. Reduce to a simmer and cook for 20 minutes, adding the remaining stock little by little as it cooks and is absorbed by the rice. You will want it to be very brothy. When the rice still has 3 minutes to go, add the shrimp and clams to the pot and continue cooking.

7. Serve in soup bowls or pasta dishes, garnished with a sprig of mint. Store any leftovers in an airtight container in the refrigerator for up to 3 days.

 WINE PAIRING
A nice godello from Galicia will pair nicely with this *arroz marinero*.

Clay Pot Pork Noodles

FIDEOS A LA CAZUELA

Prep time: 10 minutes | Cook time: 40 minutes

The Spanish way of cooking noodles (which differs greatly from the method used in Italian recipes) has been recorded since medieval times. In Spain, noodles are toasted with sautéed onions, garlic, veggies, and protein, then stewed in a rich and delicious stock. *Fideos a la cazuela*, a typical dish from Catalonia, is made with pork ribs and pancetta, but it is also delicious with fresh sausage. **SERVES 4**

8 pork ribs, separated

1 teaspoon sea salt, plus more to taste

3 garlic cloves: 1 smashed and 2 chopped

5 cups beef broth

Freshly ground black pepper

3 tablespoons extra-virgin olive oil, divided

½ cup chopped pancetta

1 small yellow onion, finely chopped

5 scallions, cut into 1½-inch pieces

1 teaspoon smoked paprika

3 tomatoes on the vine, grated on a box grater

2 cups fideo noodles or broken angel hair pasta

1. In a large soup pot, combine the ribs, salt, smashed garlic clove, and cold water to cover. Bring to a boil over high heat, then reduce the heat and simmer for 15 minutes. Remove the ribs from the pot and cut the meat off of the bones; set the meat aside and discard the bones. Set the pork broth aside.

2. In the same soup pot, combine the beef broth, 2 cups of the pork broth, and salt and pepper to taste. Heat over medium-high heat until hot, then reduce the heat to keep the broth warm.

3. In a large skillet, heat 2 tablespoons of the olive oil over medium-high heat. When hot, add the pancetta and sauté for 5 minutes, until browned. Remove the pancetta from the pan and set aside.

4. Add the remaining 1 tablespoon olive oil to the pan. When hot, add the rib meat and brown it on all sides for 8 to 10 minutes, until crispy. Mix in the pancetta.

5. Push the meat and pancetta to edges of the pan. Reduce the heat to low, add the 2 chopped garlic cloves to the center of the pan, and sauté for 2 minutes. Add the onion and a pinch of salt and sauté for 15 minutes, until soft and translucent. Move the onions to the edges of the pan, add the scallions, and sauté until soft.

Stir in the smoked paprika, grated tomatoes, and another pinch of salt and cook for 2 minutes for the tomatoes to release their liquid.

6. Stir the meats in with the vegetables, then stir in the noodles. Cook, stirring frequently, for 5 minutes to toast the noodles well. Spread the ingredients in an even layer over the pan, then cover with about 5 cups of the hot broth. Bring to a boil over high heat, then reduce the heat to low and cook for 15 minutes. Add more stock little by little as it is absorbed until the noodles are cooked. Add boiling water if more stock is needed as it is absorbed by the noodles.

7. Serve the noodles directly from the pan. Store any leftovers in an airtight container in the refrigerator for up to 4 days.

DIFFERENT SPIN

Try making this dish with fresh sausage or chorizo. Chicken or duck sausage will also work—just use chicken or vegetable broth instead of beef broth.

 WINE PAIRING

The intense flavors of this dish will pair well with the savory qualities of an oak-aged tempranillo from the Rioja appellation.

Wild Mushroom Noodles

FIDEUA DE SETAS

Prep time: 10 minutes | Cook time: 35 minutes

Easier to make than paella, *fideua* is the perfect dish for entertaining because you can casually finish the dish while enjoying a glass of wine with your guests. A popular legend says that fideua was accidentally created when a ship's cook ran out of rice while preparing paella for the crew and used pasta to complete the dish. Traditionally, fideua is made with 100-percent semolina fideo noodles, which resemble very short lengths of angel hair pasta. **SERVES 4**

¾ ounce dried porcini mushrooms

2 cups boiling water

6 cups vegetable broth

3 tablespoons extra-virgin olive oil

1 white onion, finely chopped

1 leek, white and light green parts only, well rinsed and finely chopped

2 garlic cloves, finely chopped

1 green bell pepper, finely chopped

½ teaspoon saffron threads

12 ounces white mushrooms, sliced

Sea salt

Freshly ground black pepper

12 ounces fideo noodles or broken angel hair pasta

1 tablespoon chopped fresh parsley

Aioli (page 40), for serving

1. In a small heatproof bowl, combine the porcinis and boiling water. Set aside to soak for 15 minutes. Drain the mushrooms, reserving the liquid, then chop the mushrooms.

2. In a medium pot, heat the broth over medium heat. When hot, reduce the heat to low to keep the broth hot until needed. Add the reserved mushroom soaking liquid.

3. In a large skillet, heat the olive oil over medium-low heat. When hot, add the onion, leek, and garlic and sauté for 15 minutes, until translucent. Add the bell pepper and porcinis and cook until tender, about 5 minutes. If the vegetables seem too dry, sprinkle them with a bit of broth to moisten. Add the saffron and white mushrooms and sauté for 5 minutes, until tender and lightly browned. Season with salt and black pepper.

4. Add the noodles to the pan and toast lightly, stirring often, for 5 minutes. Add enough of the broth to cover the noodles. Bring to a simmer and cook for 15 to 20 minutes, until the noodles are cooked through and tender. Add more broth to the pan as it is absorbed by the noodles. Add boiling water if more stock is needed as it is absorbed by the noodles.

5. Remove the pan from the heat, cover with a large kitchen towel, and let sit for 10 minutes.

6. Serve the noodles from the skillet, garnished with the parsley, with a bowl of aioli alongside. Store any leftovers in an airtight container in the refrigerator for up to 5 days.

SUBSTITUTION

Use any fresh mushrooms available at your local market (or a mixture) in place of the white mushrooms.

 WINE PAIRING

Try this dish with a red wine with notes of red and black fruits. I recommend the varietals monastrell and cabernet of the appellation of Jumilla.

Shrimp and Clam Noodles

FIDEOS CON GAMBAS Y ALMEJAS

Prep time: 15 minutes | Cook time: 45 minutes

This is the noodle version of brothy rice, reminiscent of Andalucía's rich maritime heritage and one of the hallmarks of the Mediterranean diet. It combines flavors and aromas of the sea with garden ingredients, olive oil, paprika, and saffron. Its flavor is boosted with *majado*, a paste made from garlic, parsley, and saffron. Majado is used in many rice dishes and stews. A large wok is perfect for making this dish if you have one. **SERVES 4**

8 tablespoons extra-virgin olive oil, divided

12 ounces medium shrimp, peeled, shells reserved

8 cups fish stock

½ cup white wine

Fine sea salt

Freshly ground black pepper

1 pound clams, such as manila or littleneck

1 cup water

2 garlic cloves

1 teaspoon saffron threads

Leaves from 7 sprigs parsley, plus 2 whole sprigs

1 yellow onion, finely chopped

1 red bell pepper, finely chopped

2 tomatoes on the vine, grated on a box grater

1 tablespoon smoked paprika

2½ cups elbow macaroni

1 lemon, halved

1. In a large soup pot, heat 2 tablespoons of the olive oil over medium-high heat. When hot, add the shrimp shells and sauté for 5 minutes. Add the stock and wine. Bring to a boil, then reduce the heat to a simmer and cook for 15 to 20 minutes to develop the flavors. Strain the broth through a fine-mesh sieve and return it to the pot. Season well with salt and black pepper. Set the pot over low heat to keep the broth hot.

2. In a large skillet, combine the clams and water. Set over medium-high heat, cover, and steam for 3 to 5 minutes, until the clams open. Discard any unopened clams. Set the opened clams aside. Strain the liquid used to steam the clams and add it to the pot with the broth. Remove the clam meat from all but 10 shells, saving those to garnish your dish.

3. To make the majado, place the garlic, saffron, and parsley leaves in a mortar and use the pestle to mix and crush them into a paste. Set aside.

4. In a large wok, deep sauté pan, or deep skillet, heat 3 table-spoons of the olive oil over medium heat. When hot, add the shrimp and sauté for 3 to 5 minutes, until pink. Remove the shrimp and set aside.

5. Add the remaining 3 tablespoons olive oil to the wok or pan. Add the onion and bell pepper and season with salt and black pepper. Cook over low heat, stirring occasionally, for 15 minutes, or until the onion is soft and translucent and the bell pepper is tender. Add the grated tomatoes and cook, stirring, for 2 minutes to release their liquid. Stir in the paprika. Bring the mixture to a boil and cook for 5 minutes. If the mixture seems dry, add just enough broth to keep it moist.

6. Stir in the macaroni and toast, stirring frequently, until golden, about 5 minutes. Increase the heat to medium-high and add half of the hot broth to cover all the ingredients. Bring to a boil and cook for 5 minutes. Stir in the majado and season with salt and black pepper. Reduce the heat to a simmer. Keep the remaining broth hot and add it little by little as the broth is absorbed by the noodles. This will take between 15 and 25 minutes.

7. When noodles are almost cooked, stir in the clam meat. To serve, lay the shrimp and whole clams in their shells on top. Garnish with the lemon halves and whole parsley sprigs. Store any leftovers in an airtight container in the refrigerator for up to 3 days.

MAKE IT MORE TRADITIONAL

A terra cotta casserole dish called a *cazuela* will make for a more authentic presentation. They are easy to find online.

 WINE PAIRING

A refreshing fruity white wine with a touch of citrus like a godello from Galicia or a verdejo from Rueda pairs nicely with this dish.

Tomato and Chorizo Penne

MACARONES CON TOMATE Y CHORIZO

Prep time: 10 minutes | Cook time: 20 minutes

Treat your friends and family to some traditional Spanish comfort food. The simplest version of Spanish "mac 'n' cheese" is made with two favorite Spanish ingredients: tomato and chorizo. You can use homemade tomato sauce and authentic Spanish chorizo or a good-quality ready-made sauce and hickory-smoked Portuguese-style linguiça, available at most supermarkets. **SERVES 6**

Sea salt

12 ounces penne pasta

½ pound chorizo, chopped

1 tablespoon extra-virgin olive oil

3 cups Spanish Tomato Sauce (page 59)

⅓ cup red wine

1 teaspoon fresh or dried thyme

2 teaspoons fresh or dried oregano, divided

1 cup shredded whole-milk mozzarella cheese

½ cup grated Parmesan cheese

1 tablespoon chiffonade-cut fresh basil (ribbons)

1. Preheat the oven to 400°F.

2. Bring a large pot of salted water to a boil. Add the penne and cook until al dente according to package directions. Drain well.

3. Heat a small skillet over medium-high heat. When hot, add the chorizo and olive oil and fry until the sausage is crispy. Set aside.

4. In a medium sauté pan or skillet, heat the tomato sauce over medium heat. When hot, add the wine, thyme, 1 teaspoon of the oregano, and salt to taste. Cook for about 3 minutes to burn off the alcohol. Add the chorizo and mix well.

5. In a small bowl, combine the mozzarella, Parmesan, basil, and remaining 1 teaspoon oregano. Mix well.

6. Stir the drained pasta into the tomato sauce. Transfer to a 9-by-13-inch baking dish. Spread the cheese mixture over the top.

7. Bake for 15 minutes, or until the cheese melts. Serve hot. Store any leftovers in an airtight container in the refrigerator for up to 4 days.

DIFFERENT SPINS

Use any good melting cheese such as Fontina, Gouda (not aged), Havarti, Manchego, Monterey Jack, or pecorino instead of the mozzarella. Or add about 8 slices of fresh mozzarella or burrata for extra creaminess.

 WINE PAIRING

This dish will pair best with a fruity and full-bodied garnacha from Aragon.

CHAPTER SIX

---⊙---

Meats and Seafood

Spain is famous for its quality and variety of seafood, which plays a prominent role in every region's cuisine. But the country's meat and poultry dishes are just as important. For centuries, Muslim, Jewish, and Christian settlers consumed lamb in the Iberian Peninsula, greatly influencing the Spanish food culture. Iberian pork produces one of Spain's culinary jewels: *jamón ibérico de bellota*, acorn-fed cured Iberian ham. This chapter will introduce you to some of Spain's most delectable meat and seafood classics.

Chicken in Tomato-Pepper Sauce (page 122)

Meatballs in Grandma's Sauce

ALBÓNDIGAS EN SALSA DE LA ABUELA

Prep time: 20 minutes | Cook time: 40 minutes

Albóndigas are part of the culinary inheritance from the Al-Andalus, the Muslim kingdom that occupied the Iberian Peninsula during the Middle Ages. The word *albóngidas* comes from the Arabic *al-búndiga*, which is *la bola* in Spanish, and "ball" in English. In Spain, you can find them as a tapa at your local bar, but they are an all-time favorite at every home with Grandma's traditional meatball recipe. Serve them with potatoes: crispy oven-roasted, fried, cubed, or mashed. **SERVES 4**

4 garlic cloves: 1 sliced, 3 finely chopped	4 ounces ground pork	1 tablespoon fine dried bread crumbs
Leaves from 5 parsley sprigs, leaves picked, plus 4 whole sprigs, chopped	Sea salt	1 cup all-purpose flour
	Freshly ground black pepper	¼ cup extra-virgin olive oil, plus 3 tablespoons
1 cup fino sherry	2 large eggs, beaten	1 large yellow onion, sliced
1 pound ground beef (80/20)	1 medium yellow onion, finely chopped	1 cup beef broth

1. In a mortar, combine the sliced garlic clove, parsley leaves, and sherry and crush with the pestle to form a paste (this mixture is called a *majado*). (Alternatively, place the ingredients in a small bowl and use a stick blender to combine them.) Set aside.

2. In a large bowl, combine the ground beef and pork. Season with salt and pepper and mix to combine. Add the eggs, white onion, one-third of the chopped garlic, the chopped parsley, and the bread crumbs and mix well.

3. Roll the mixture into 1½-inch balls. Place the flour in a shallow bowl and coat each meatball lightly in the flour. Set the meatballs aside on a sheet of wax paper.

4. In a large sauté pan or skillet, heat ¼ cup of the olive oil over medium-high heat. When hot, add the meatballs and cook for about 5 minutes, browning them on all sides. The exterior should be browned, but the meatballs should be rare inside. Be careful not to overcook. Transfer the meatballs to a plate and set aside.

5. Reduce the heat to low and add the remaining 3 tablespoons olive oil. When hot, add the yellow onion and remaining chopped garlic and sauté for 15 to 20 minutes, until soft and translucent.

6. Add the broth and the majado. Bring to a boil over medium-high heat, then reduce to a simmer and cook for 5 minutes, or until the sauce reaches your desired consistency. Taste and season with salt and pepper, if needed.

7. Transfer the sauce to a blender and blend until smooth. Return the sauce to the pan, place over medium-high heat, and add the meatballs. Cook for 3 to 5 minutes, until the sauce warms and the meatballs are cooked through. Do not let the sauce boil or you will have dry meatballs.

8. Serve hot. Store leftovers in an airtight container in the refrigerator for up to 5 days.

DIFFERENT SPIN

Use a sweet white wine in place of the sherry.

 WINE PAIRING

A red wine aged in oak for 12 months and with a mix of tempranillo, merlot, cabernet sauvignon, and syrah varietals will pair well with this dish.

Sailor-Style Clams

ALMEJAS A LA MARINERA

Prep time: 20 minutes | Cook time: 30 minutes

This dish originated in Galicia's Rias Baixas region. It is traditionally made and served in a *cazuela de barro*, a terra cotta casserole dish. **SERVES 4**

1½ cups white wine, divided

1 pound clams, manila or littleneck, rinsed in cold water

1 bay leaf

½ cup extra-virgin olive oil

2 medium yellow onions, finely chopped

2 garlic cloves, minced

1 teaspoon sea salt

½ cup water

2 tablespoons Spanish Tomato Sauce (page 59)

1 tablespoon smoked paprika

Pinch red pepper flakes, or to taste

1 teaspoon all-purpose flour (optional)

¼ cup finely chopped fresh parsley

1. In a medium soup pot, bring ½ cup of the wine to a boil over medium-high heat. Add the clams and bay leaf. Cover and steam for 2 minutes, until the clams open. Using a slotted spoon, remove the clams and set aside. Discard any unopened clams. Pour the liquid from the pot into a bowl and set aside.

2. In the same soup pot, heat the olive oil over medium heat. When hot, add the onions, garlic, and salt and sauté for 15 to 20 minutes, until the onions are light brown in color. When the pan starts to get dry as the onions cook, add the water little by little so the onions do not burn.

3. Add the tomato sauce, smoked paprika, and pepper flakes and mix for 1 minute. Add the flour (if using), mixing well to ensure it cooks but being careful that it does not burn. This will thicken your sauce. Add the remaining 1 cup wine and the reserved clam cooking liquid. Cook for 10 minutes.

4. Return the clams to the pot and cook, stirring for 2 minutes to heat through.

5. Transfer to a bowl, sprinkle with the parsley, and serve. Store leftovers in an airtight container in the refrigerator for up to 3 days.

REGIONAL VARIATION

For an Asturian version, omit the tomato sauce.

 WINE PAIRING

Enjoy this dish with a Spanish white wine of the godello varietal, or try it with an albariño, which may be easier to find.

Andalucían Fried Marinated Mahimahi

BIENMESABE

Prep time: 5 minutes, plus 6 hours to marinate | Cook time: 15 minutes

Bienmesabe (which means "it tastes good to me") is a delicious representation of Andalucía's famous fried fish. It is usually made with *cazón*, a small shark (and is also known as *cazón en adobo*), but works well with mahimahi (as called for here) or swordfish. Though quick to cook, the fish has to marinate for at least 6 hours to get the fullest flavor. Accompany this dish with *asadillo de pimientos andaluz* (Roasted Pepper Salad, page 42) for a full Andalucían experience. **SERVES 4**

---

1 teaspoon ground cumin

1 teaspoon smoked paprika

1 teaspoon dried oregano

½ teaspoon sea salt

¼ cup sherry vinegar

1 pound mahimahi, cut into 2-inch pieces

2 bay leaves

1 cup all-purpose flour

2 cups extra-virgin olive oil

Lemon slices, for garnish

1. In a large glass or other nonmetal bowl, mix together the cumin, paprika, oregano, salt, and vinegar. Add the mahimahi. Cut each bay leaf into 3 pieces and add them to the bowl. Mix well and add just enough water so the fish is covered. Cover the bowl with plastic wrap and refrigerate for at least 6 hours, or up to overnight.

2. Drain the fish and discard the marinade. Place the flour on a plate. Using tongs, coat each piece of fish well on all sides. Place the fish in a sieve, a few pieces at a time, and shake off any excess flour.

3. Line a plate with paper towels. In a saucepan no wider than 8 inches, heat the olive oil over high heat. When hot, work in batches to fry the fish for 3 to 4 minutes, until golden brown. Transfer the fish to the paper towel–lined plate to drain any excess oil.

4. Serve on a platter, garnished with lemon slices. Store leftovers in an airtight container in the refrigerator for up to 2 days. The fish will remain moist and tender inside.

 WINE PAIRING

Pair this dish with a riesling and you will be pleasantly surprised! The wine's subtle sweetness contrasts well with the marinade's acidity. Try a manzanilla sherry to complete the meal.

Cod with Raisins and Pine Nuts

BACALAO CON PASAS Y PIÑONES

Prep time: 10 minutes | Cook time: 30 minutes

Cod is a favorite fish in Spain and can be found throughout several regions and in many different recipes. This dish, also known as *bacalao a la catalana* (Catalan-style cod), is traditionally made with salt cod (see Tip), but this version uses fresh cod to make things easier and quicker. **SERVES 4**

¼ cup plus 5 tablespoons extra-virgin olive oil, divided

2 (½-inch-thick) slices baguette, sliced on the diagonal

2 pounds cod fillets

Sea salt

Freshly ground black pepper

1 cup all-purpose flour

1 medium yellow onion, thinly sliced

4 tomatoes on the vine, grated on a box grater

1 cup water

1 tablespoon pine nuts

1 tablespoon raisins

2 tablespoons chopped fresh parsley

1. In a nonstick medium sauté pan or skillet, heat 5 tablespoons of the olive oil over medium-high heat. When hot, add the bread slices and fry them for 2 minutes per side, until crisp on both sides. Set aside, leaving the oil in the pan.

2. Season the cod with salt and pepper. Place the flour on a plate and coat both sides of the fillets in it.

3. Set the pan over medium heat. When the oil is hot, add the cod and pan-fry for 5 minutes per side, until opaque and flaky. Transfer to a plate.

4. Reduce the heat to medium-low and add the remaining ¼ cup olive oil. When hot, add the onion and sauté for 15 minutes, or until browned. If the pan gets dry as the onion cooks, add a little water.

5. Add the grated tomatoes, reduce the heat to low, and simmer for about 3 minutes to release their liquid. Add the 1 cup water, the pine nuts, and the raisins. Bring to a boil over medium-high heat, then reduce to a simmer and cook for 10 minutes.

6. Crush the fried bread and add it to the pan to thicken the sauce. Add the cod and season with salt and pepper.

7. Serve on a platter or in a *cazuela*, garnished with the parsley. Store leftovers in an airtight container in the refrigerator for up to 3 days.

MAKE IT MORE TRADITIONAL

Using salt cod gives the sauce a more emulsified texture. To use salt cod, it first has to be soaked to remove some of the salt: Cover the cod with cool water and refrigerate for 24 hours, changing the water every 8 hours. Fresh black cod can also be used and is delicious in this recipe.

 WINE PAIRING

This dish pairs well with a sparkling or still rosé. Look for a rosé from Navarra or a rosé cava from Catalonia.

Sea Bass on Its Back

BESUGO A LA ESPALDA

Prep time: 5 minutes | Cook time: 15 minutes

This traditional dish, also known as *besugo a la donostiarra*, which means "red sea bream from San Sebastián," can be made with any type of flaky white-fleshed fish fillet, but it is best when the skin is left on. It is presented *a la espalda* (on its back), served open-faced with the sauce poured over it. This dish pairs well with boiled peeled potatoes seasoned with flaky sea salt, black pepper, and extra-virgin olive oil, or with Baker's Potatoes (page 52). **SERVES 4**

---

4 skin-on sea bass or branzino fillets (about 4 ounces each)

Sea salt

Freshly ground black pepper

8 tablespoons extra-virgin olive oil, divided

4 garlic cloves, sliced

Red pepper flakes

¼ cup fresh parsley leaves, finely chopped

½ cup dry white wine

¼ cup sherry vinegar or red wine vinegar

Flaky sea salt

1. Pat the fish skin dry with a paper towel. Season both sides of the fish with salt and black pepper.

2. In a large nonstick skillet, heat 2 tablespoons of the olive oil over medium-high heat. When hot, add the fish, skin-side down, and cook 5 to 7 minutes (depending on the size of the fillets), until the edge of the skin turns golden brown. Carefully flip the fillets over and cook for 2 minutes more, until flaky. Transfer the fish to a platter.

3. In a small skillet, heat the remaining 6 tablespoons olive oil over medium heat. When hot, add the garlic and pepper flakes to taste and sauté for about 1 minute to lightly brown the garlic, being careful not to burn it. Add the parsley, wine, and vinegar and bring to a boil. Reduce the heat, cover, and simmer for 5 minutes.

4. Pour the sauce over the fish and serve immediately, sprinkled with flaky sea salt. Store leftovers in an airtight container in the refrigerator for up to 3 days.

DIFFERENT SPIN

This recipe works well with any white-fleshed flaky fish, but salmon will work well, too. Traditionally the skin is left on the fillets, but it is delicious without the skin as well. Just shorten the cooking time on the first side to 5 minutes.

 WINE PAIRING

This dish pairs well with a white garnacha or viura from La Rioja.

Squid in Onion Sauce

CALAMARES ENCEBOLLADOS

Prep time: 10 minutes | Cook time: 45 minutes

Legend has it that there was a surge in the squid population in the 20th century in Getaria, a town on the Basque coast, and a chef who was tired of always making calamari in squid ink decided to innovate. This recipe was the result, and it has become a star dish of Basque cuisine. The calamari are cooked smothered in a divine golden-brown caramelized onion sauce. It is delicious and easy to make, but to save time you must buy your squid already cleaned! **SERVES 4**

⅓ cup extra-virgin olive oil

4 garlic cloves, sliced

2 medium yellow onions, coarsely chopped

1 teaspoon sea salt, plus more for seasoning

½ teaspoon freshly ground black pepper, plus more for seasoning

2 bay leaves

⅓ cup water, as needed

¾ cup white wine

2 pounds calamari rings and tentacles

Cooked white rice, for serving

1. In a large pot, heat the olive oil over medium heat. When hot, add the garlic and cook for 1 minute to lightly brown. Add the onions, salt, pepper, and bay leaves, mixing well. Cover the pot and cook until liquid releases, about 5 minutes. Uncover and sauté the onions, stirring occasionally, for 15 to 20 minutes, until they are golden brown. Add water, if needed, little by little until the golden color is obtained.

2. Increase the heat to high and add the wine. Cook, stirring occasionally, for 2 minutes to burn off the alcohol.

3. Add the calamari and sauté for 2 to 3 minutes, until it begins to turn opaque. Reduce the heat to medium, cover the pot, and simmer for 20 minutes, until the calamari becomes tender.

4. Serve in a wide bowl, accompanied by white rice to soak up the caramelized onion sauce. This dish is even better the following day. Store leftovers in an airtight container in the refrigerator for up to 3 days. You can also freeze it for up to 1 month.

REGIONAL VARIATION

In Cádiz, Andalucía, world-famous for their unique method of tuna fishing (called *almadraba*), they make this dish with tuna instead of squid. Use 1¼ pounds fresh bluefin tuna. Once you add it to the pot, let it simmer for just a few minutes to avoid overcooking it.

 WINE PAIRING

Pair this dish with a Spanish sauvignon blanc, which is produced in various regions: Rueda, Penedès, Valencia, Mallorca, Castilla y Léon, La Mancha, and Navarra.

Squid in Ink Sauce

CALAMARES EN SU TINTA

Prep time: 15 minutes | Cook time: 1 hour

Although considered a Basque delicacy, this dish is a treasured comfort food throughout Spain. You will find it as a tapa at bars or made into croquettes. More upscale versions can include calamari stuffed with garlic, oregano, leeks, carrots, chopped tentacles, Serrano ham, or even crab. **SERVES 4**

1 cup extra-virgin olive oil

4 medium yellow onions, chopped

2 garlic cloves, peeled

1 tablespoon Spanish Tomato Sauce (page 59; optional)

2 (4-gram) pouches squid ink

2 pounds calamari rings

1 cup red wine

1 cup water, as needed

Sea salt

Freshly ground black pepper

Finely chopped fresh parsley

Cooked white rice, for serving

1. In a large pot, heat the olive oil over medium heat. When hot, reduce the heat to low and add the onions, mixing well. Cover the pot and cook the onions until the liquid releases, about 5 minutes. Uncover and cook for 15 minutes, until the onions become soft and translucent.

2. Meanwhile, place the garlic, tomato sauce (if using), and squid ink in a mortar and crush and mix well with the pestle. Set aside.

3. Add the calamari and wine to the onions and simmer for 2 to 3 minutes to burn off the alcohol. Add the garlic mixture to the pan and mix well. Cover and simmer for 40 minutes. Add up to 1 cup water as needed little by little if the pot starts to become dry. Taste and season with salt and pepper.

4. Transfer to a wide bowl or *cazuela* and garnish with parsley. Serve with rice. Store leftovers in an airtight container in the refrigerator for up to 3 days.

TECHNIQUE TIP

Though it will take more time, it's even easier to put all of the ingredients (except for the salt and pepper) in a pot, bring to a boil over medium heat, reduce the heat to low, and simmer for 2 hours. Season with salt and pepper to taste before serving.

 WINE PAIRING

Try an albariño from Galicia or a red tempranillo from La Rioja.

Vine Shoot–Grilled Lamb Chops

CHULETILLAS DE CORDERO AL SARMIENTO

Prep time: 5 minutes | Cook time: 15 minutes

A classic Spanish method of cooking lamb chops is to grill them over tied vine shoots that have burnt down to hot embers. In this recipe, a very hot cast-iron skillet stands in for a grill and vine shoots (impossible to find unless you live near a vineyard). Enjoy the lamb chops with Roasted Pepper Salad from Andalucía (page 42), Romesco Sauce (page 54), or Spicy Mojo Sauce (page 51). **SERVES 4**

16 lamb rib chops (see Tip)
Flaky sea salt
Freshly ground
    black pepper

2 teaspoons finely chopped
    fresh rosemary leaves
2 teaspoons fresh
    thyme leaves

⅓ cup extra-virgin olive oil
¼ cup red wine, preferably
    tempranillo

1. Season the lamb chops with salt and pepper. Sprinkle with the rosemary and thyme.

2. In a 12-inch cast-iron skillet, heat the olive oil over high heat. When very hot (it must be very hot to achieve a juicy interior and a crispy exterior on the meat), add about half the lamb chops (or whatever will fit in a single layer) and cook for 2 to 3 minutes. Turn the chops over and cook for 2 to 3 minutes on the other side. Flip the chops over and cook for 2 more minutes on each side for an extra-crispy exterior. Repeat with the remaining chops

3. Return all the chops to the pan. Pour the wine over the lamb chops and cook for 1 minute.

4. Serve on a platter. Store leftovers in an airtight container in the refrigerator for up to 3 days.

TECHNIQUE TIP

It is important to buy the smallest lamb chops available. In Spain, suckling lamb chops are used, which have a milder flavor. The younger the lamb, the lighter the flavor.

 WINE PAIRING

Serve with a tempranillo from La Rioja or a rosé of tempranillo and garnacha varietals from Navarra.

Roasted Leg of Lamb

CORDERO ASADO

Prep time: 5 minutes | Cook time: 2 hours

Roasted lamb, traditionally enjoyed during festivities and holidays, is the dish most typical of Castilian cuisine. It is often roasted with just salt and water and is always served with potatoes and a salad of lettuce, tomatoes, and sweet onions. Look for a smaller leg of lamb, which will give a more subtle and elegant flavor to your roast. In Spain, suckling or young lamb is usually used. **SERVES 6**

Sea salt

Freshly ground
   black pepper

1 cup extra-virgin olive
   oil, divided

4 large Yukon Gold
   potatoes, sliced
   ¼ inch thick

16 garlic cloves:
   10 unpeeled, 6 peeled

1 (3-pound) boneless
   leg of lamb

½ cup fresh parsley leaves,
   finely chopped

2 tablespoons fresh
   rosemary leaves, plus
   4 rosemary sprigs

1 cup white wine

1 cup water

1. Preheat the oven to 390°F.

2. Sprinkle salt and pepper over the bottom of a large roasting pan. Drizzle ¼ cup of the olive oil over the bottom of the pan. Spread the sliced potatoes over the bottom of the pan and mix the 10 unpeeled garlic cloves among them.

3. Season the lamb with salt and pepper and rub with ¼ cup of the olive oil to coat all sides. Place the lamb on top of the potatoes.

4. In a mortar, combine the 6 peeled garlic cloves, the parsley, rosemary leaves, and a couple spoonfuls of the wine and crush with the pestle. Transfer to a medium bowl and add the remaining wine and ½ cup olive oil. Add the 1 cup water and mix well. Pour the liquid over the lamb and the potatoes.

5. Roast the lamb for 1½ hours, basting it every 20 minutes with the juices it releases. Add water to the pan if needed for the basting liquid. Increase the oven temperature to 420°F and roast for 30 minutes to brown the exterior of the lamb. For medium-rare, the internal temperature should register between 130° and 135°F on an instant-read thermometer.

6. Remove the lamb from the oven and let sit for 15 minutes before slicing. Check that the potatoes are cooked through. Leave them in the oven if additional time is needed. Serve on a large platter with the potatoes, garnished with the rosemary sprigs. Store leftovers in an airtight container in the refrigerator for up to 5 days.

TECHNIQUE TIP

Use your leftover lamb to make a lamb *chilindrón* following the recipe for Chicken in Tomato-Pepper Sauce (page 122). Use cubes of roast lamb in place of the chicken called for, but only sauté it for about 5 minutes.

 WINE PAIRING

This dish pairs well with a Ribera del Duero, the most prestigious wine region in Castilla y Léon.

Salt-Roasted Sea Bass

LUBINA A LA SAL

Prep time: 5 minutes | Cook time: 20 minutes

This dish is just about everywhere in beach restaurants on Andalucía's Costa del Sol. Cooking the whole fish in a "shell" of salt is the best way to enjoy the fish's natural flavor. The salt crust maintains the fish's moisture, giving it a perfect flaky texture without making it too salty. **SERVES 4**

1 whole sea bass (2 pounds), cleaned, with skin and head on

4 pounds coarse sea salt
¼ cup water

Aioli (page 40), mayonnaise, or extra-virgin olive oil, for serving

1. Position a rack in the center of the oven and preheat the oven to 350°F.

2. Rinse the fish inside and out and pat dry with paper towels.

3. In a baking pan big enough to accommodate the whole fish, create a bed of coarse sea salt using one-third of the salt and lay the fish on top. Mix the remaining salt with the water and cover the fish entirely. Pat it down to compress the salt onto the fish, which will create a good crust and seal the fish.

4. Bake the fish for 20 minutes.

5. Remove the fish from the oven and immediately crack the crust open, removing the salt entirely. Discard the salt crust. Cut through the skin alongside the spine to open the fish. Separate the meat from the skin and transfer the fish to a warm platter.

6. Serve with aioli or mayonnaise, or sprinkle with extra-virgin olive oil.

TECHNIQUE TIP

At your local fish market, request to have the scales and guts removed from the fish but the head left on.

SUBSTITUTION

It is best to use a large white-fleshed fish such as sea bass, turbot, or snapper, but sea bream and branzino will work, too. You can also roast two smaller fish together. For every pound of fish, you will need 2 pounds salt. Bake the fish at 350°F for 10 minutes per pound.

 WINE PAIRING

Pair it with a chilled Fino sherry from Jerez de la Frontera, readily available in North America.

Garlic Chicken
POLLO AL AJILLO

Prep time: 15 minutes | Cook time: 25 minutes

Pollo al ajillo is an easy dish to love with its perfectly browned chicken, juicy as can be, and mouthwatering garlic sauce that you will surely want to dip your bread in. **SERVES 4**

⅓ cup extra-virgin olive oil

12 garlic cloves, peeled

2 pounds boneless, skinless chicken thighs, cut into 2-inch pieces

Sea salt

Freshly ground black pepper

1 cup white wine

1 parsley sprig, for garnish

Rice or French fries, for serving

1. In a large skillet, heat the olive oil over medium heat. When hot, add the garlic and sauté for 5 minutes, until browned.

2. Meanwhile, season the chicken with 1 teaspoon each of salt and pepper.

3. Using tongs or a slotted spoon, remove the garlic and set aside. Increase the heat to medium-high and add the chicken. Cook until browned on both sides, 10 to 15 minutes.

4. Add the wine and return the garlic to the pan. Cover and cook for 15 minutes to make the sauce and garlic cloves creamy. Season to taste with salt and pepper.

5. Serve the chicken on a plate with the sauce and garlic cloves poured over it. Garnish with the parsley and accompany with rice or French fries. Store leftovers in an airtight container in the refrigerator for up to 5 days.

REGIONAL VARIATION

To add a taste of Andalucía, substitute fino sherry for the wine.

DIFFERENT SPINS

Add a pinch of red pepper flakes for a hint of spice. And if you want to have more sauce, add ½ cup chicken broth 5 minutes after adding the wine.

Halibut in Green Sauce with Clams

MERLUZA EN SALSA VERDE CON ALMEJAS

Prep time: 10 minutes | Cook time: 20 minutes

One of Spain's most popular seafood dishes, this traditional Basque favorite is made here with halibut, which best resembles the Spanish *merluza*. It is often garnished with hard-boiled eggs and white asparagus and presented in a terra cotta *cazuela*. **SERVES 4**

---

7 tablespoons extra-virgin olive oil, divided

4 halibut steaks (8 ounces each), cut 2 inches thick

4 garlic cloves, sliced

1½ teaspoons all-purpose flour

½ cup dry white wine

2¼ cups clam broth or fish stock

12 clams, such as manila or littleneck

1 cup green peas (optional)

2 tablespoons finely chopped fresh parsley

1. In a medium skillet, heat ¼ cup of the olive oil over medium heat. When hot, add the fish and brown for about 5 minutes on each side. Transfer to a plate and set aside.

2. In the same skillet, heat 3 tablespoons of the olive oil over medium heat. When hot, add the garlic and cook for 1 minute to lightly brown. Remove the pan from the heat and add the flour, whisking for 1 minute. Whisk in the wine, then the broth. Set the pan over high heat and cook, whisking, for 2 minutes to thicken the sauce.

3. Add the clams, peas (if using), and fish. Shake the pan and cook for 6 minutes, until the clams open. Discard any unopened clams. Finish by sprinkling the parsley over the top.

4. Serve the fish in a deep serving dish or in individual bowls, topped with clams, peas, and sauce. Store leftovers in an airtight container in the refrigerator for up to 3 days.

MAKE IT MORE TRADITIONAL
Garnish the dish with halved or quartered hard-boiled eggs and white asparagus.

 WINE PAIRING
This dish pairs well with an albariño, verdejo, or chardonnay.

Rock Cod with Txakoli
RODABALLO AL TXAKOLI

Prep time: 10 minutes | Cook time: 30 minutes

Txakoli is the wine of the Basques. It is popularly consumed in every *caserio* (country farmhouse). It is a dry, slightly sparkling, usually white wine that is often used to cook fish. **SERVES 4**

---

1 cup extra-virgin olive oil, divided

2 medium yellow onions, finely chopped

3 garlic cloves, minced

Sea salt

Freshly ground black pepper

2 pounds rock cod fillets

16 clams, such as manila or littleneck (optional)

1 cup dry white wine, divided

¼ cup apple cider vinegar

8 medium shrimp, peeled and deveined (optional)

1 cup green peas

¼ cup finely chopped fresh parsley

1. In a large nonstick skillet, heat ⅓ cup of the olive oil over medium-low heat. When hot, add the onions and garlic and sauté for 10 to 15 minutes, until soft and translucent. Season with salt and pepper and transfer to a bowl.

2. Season the fish with salt and pepper and cut each fillet in half. In the same skillet, heat the remaining ⅔ cup olive oil over medium heat. When hot, add the cod and brown on both sides, about 5 minutes total.

3. Return the onions and garlic to the pan and add the clams (if using) and ½ cup of the wine. Cook for about 5 minutes, shaking the pan constantly. The constant motion will allow the cod to almost emulsify with the oil. Turn the fish over and add the vinegar and remaining ½ cup wine.

4. Add the shrimp (if using), peas, and parsley and cook, shaking the pan occasionally, for about 5 minutes to thicken the sauce.

5. Transfer the fish to a serving dish and spoon the sauce, clams, and shrimp over it. Store leftovers in an airtight container in the refrigerator for up to 3 days.

MAKE IT MORE TRADITIONAL

This dish would traditionally be made with salt cod. To use salt cod, first cover it with cold water and refrigerate it for 24 hours, changing the water about every 8 hours (alternatively, run it under cold water and then quickly wash it in boiling water 3 or 4 times).

 WINE PAIRING

Try this dish with Ameztoi Txakolina Rosé.

Chicken in Tomato-Pepper Sauce

POLLO AL CHILINDRÓN

Prep time: 10 minutes | Cook time: 50 minutes

Chilindrón refers to the perfect combination of three basic ingredients in Spanish cuisine: red bell pepper, onion, and tomato. The name comes from the winning hand—"jack, horse, king"—in an old card game (played with the traditional deck of Spanish playing cards) called *chilindrón*. Common to both Aragón and Navarra (where they add green bell peppers and often make the dish with rabbit), this is the Aragonian version. Serve with roasted potatoes or white rice. **SERVES 4**

4 tablespoons extra-virgin olive oil, divided

4 garlic cloves: 2 crushed, 2 sliced

2 pounds boneless, skinless chicken thighs, cut into 2-inch pieces

1 red onion, julienned

2 red bell peppers, julienned

1 cup water, divided

1 cup dry white wine, plus 2 tablespoons

½ cup diced prosciutto

1 teaspoon smoked paprika

4 tomatoes on the vine, grated on a box grater

½ teaspoon fresh thyme leaves

Leaves from 1 rosemary sprig

Sea salt

Freshly ground black pepper

1. In a large pot, heat 2 tablespoons of the olive oil over medium-high heat. When hot, add the 2 crushed garlic cloves and sauté for 1 to 2 minutes to lightly brown. Remove and set aside.

2. In the same pan over medium-high heat, add the chicken and brown on all sides, 10 to 15 minutes. Transfer the chicken to a platter and set aside.

3. In the same pot, heat the remaining 2 tablespoons olive oil over medium heat. When hot, add the onion and bell peppers and sauté for about 15 minutes, until soft and translucent. Add up to ¼ cup water little by little if the onion starts to burn.

4. Add the sliced garlic cloves and brown for 5 more minutes. Add 1 cup of the wine and cook for about 5 minutes to burn off the alcohol. Add the prosciutto, browned chicken, smoked paprika, and grated tomatoes and mix well.

5. In a mortar, combine the browned crushed garlic, thyme, rosemary leaves, remaining 2 tablespoons wine, salt and pepper to taste, and just enough water to facilitate crushing the mixture into a paste with the pestle. Add the paste and the remaining ¾ cup water to the pot and stir to combine. Bring to a boil, then reduce the heat and simmer for 20 to 25 minutes to combine all of the flavors.

6. Serve hot. Store leftovers in an airtight container in the refrigerator for 3 days or freeze in a freezer bag or airtight container for up to 1 month.

DIFFERENT SPIN

For lamb chilindrón, substitute cubes of lamb for the chicken.

 WINE PAIRING

A pinot noir from the Somontano appellation in Aragón complements the zesty flavors of this dish.

Scallops with Cured Ham

VIERAS CON JAMÓN

Prep time: 15 minutes | Cook time: 20 minutes

The yellow scallop shell is the iconic symbol of the pilgrimage to Santiago de Compostela and can be found on trees and cobblestone walls along the *camino* (route). This scallop dish is traditionally served in Galicia on a scallop shell with oven-toasted bread crumbs and bay scallops. This version can be served as a first course or an entrée. **SERVES 4**

⅓ cup extra-virgin olive oil

2 medium yellow onions, finely chopped

¼ cup chopped fresh parsley

¼ teaspoon saffron threads

12 large sea scallops

¼ cup chopped Serrano ham or prosciutto

1 cup white wine

1. In a medium sauté pan or skillet, heat the olive oil over medium heat. When hot, add the onions and sauté until they become soft and translucent, about 15 minutes. Add the parsley and cook, stirring occasionally, for 10 minutes, until the onions begin to brown. If the pan becomes too dry, add a little water as needed. Mix in the saffron, which will add color to your sautéed onions.

2. Add the scallops and reduce the heat to low. Sauté, stirring occasionally, for 2 minutes. Add the ham and cook, stirring to release its fat, for about 2 minutes. Pour in the wine and simmer until the sauce reduces, about 10 minutes.

3. Serve the scallops in a bowl with the sauce poured over the top. Store leftovers in an airtight container in the refrigerator for up to 3 days.

REGIONAL VARIATION

Serve this dish as a tapa or starter in a ceramic scallop shell or small vessel with toasted bread crumbs garnished with fresh parsley, and you will transform it into *vieras a la gallega*, or Galician scallops.

 WINE PAIRING

For this dish, pour an oak-aged godello from Valdeorras appellation or a sauvignon blanc from the Penedès DO.

CHAPTER SEVEN

―――――――○―――――――

Desserts and Drinks

In Spain, a meal is not complete until you have dessert, whether a piece of seasonal fruit or one of Grandma's secret recipes. Likewise, Spaniards love their drinks and have put their own unique spin on several thirst-quenchers. This chapter is a compilation of my family's favorite Spanish desserts, which may even suit your fancy as an afternoon treat or a breakfast, for those of you with a sweet tooth. There are also a few typical drinks that are part of the Spanish lifestyle. As the charming Spanish toast says, "*Arriba, abajo, al centro, y adentro!*" Up, down, to the center, and inside!

Churros with Hot Chocolate (page 132)

Rice Pudding

ARROZ CON LECHE

Prep time: 5 minutes, plus 2 hours to chill | Cook time: 1 hour 30 minutes

Rice pudding is omnipresent in Spain's dessert culture. It is originally from the region of Asturias in northern Spain. This dessert is labor-intensive, so prepare for a worthwhile arm workout! It is also delicious sprinkled with ½ cup of sugar burnt with a kitchen blowtorch or under the broiler. **SERVES 6**

---

1 cup short-grain rice, such as bomba

1 quart whole milk

1 cinnamon stick

Grated zest of 1 lemon

Grated zest of 1 orange

1½ cups sugar

1 teaspoon ground cinnamon

1. In a large nonstick pot, combine the rice, milk, cinnamon stick, lemon zest, and orange zest. Bring to a boil over high heat, then reduce the heat to a simmer and cook for 1 hour, stirring every 10 to 15 minutes to prevent sticking.

2. Add the sugar and cook, stirring constantly, for 30 minutes more.

3. Pour into a bowl and let cool to room temperature. When cool, sprinkle with the ground cinnamon. You can serve this at room temperature, but most prefer it chilled; refrigerate until chilled, 2 to 3 hours.

4. Serve it into individual bowls or glasses with a teaspoon. Store leftovers in an airtight container in the refrigerator for up to 5 days.

SUBSTITUTION

If you can't source Spanish short-grain bomba rice, use sushi rice.

 WINE PAIRING

A moscatel with citric and white fruit notes will pair nicely with the rice pudding.

Chocolate Crème Anglaise with Raspberries

NATILLAS DE CHOCOLATE CON FRAMBUESAS

Prep time: 5 minutes, plus 2 hours to chill | Cook time: 20 minutes

This is a take on the traditional vanilla and cinnamon *natillas*, a favorite in Spain. It's especially good topped with fresh raspberries, which contrast divinely with the dark chocolate. **SERVES 8**

---

1 quart whole milk	6 large egg yolks
8 ounces dark chocolate	1¼ cups sugar
(63% cacao),	1 tablespoon cornstarch
coarsely chopped	Raspberries, for serving

1. In a large saucepan, combine the milk and chocolate. Bring just to a boil over medium-low heat.

2. Meanwhile, in a large bowl, beat the egg yolks with the sugar. Beat in the cornstarch.

3. When the milk just begins to boil, remove the pan from the heat. Slowly pour it into the egg yolk mixture little by little, whisking constantly, until fully combined. Pour the mixture back into the saucepan.

4. Place the pan over medium heat and whisk constantly until the mixture thickens, 5 minutes or less. Be careful not to let it boil.

5. Remove the pan from the heat and pour the crème anglaise into a bowl. Let cool to room temperature, then cover the bowl with plastic wrap and refrigerate for at least 2 hours to chill.

6. Serve in individual bowls topped with raspberries. Store leftovers in an airtight container in the refrigerator for up to 5 days.

REGIONAL VARIATION

In Spain, natillas are traditionally served with Maria biscuits. If you can find them at your local grocery market, try dipping them into the chocolate crème!

 WINE PAIRING

Pedro Ximénez, an intensely sweet, dark, dessert sherry, will pair nicely with this dessert and so will a port.

Spanish Cake Roll

BRAZO GITANO

Prep time: 20 minutes | Cook time: 8 minutes

There are several popular legends about the origins of this dessert. Some say it is over 100 years old and comes from Barcelona, and others say that it dates back to the Egyptians in the Middle Ages—who knows which one is true. What is certain is that it is an easy-to-make dessert with numerous filling possibilities. **SERVES 8**

FOR THE CAKE ROLL

3 large eggs, separated

½ cup powdered sugar

¼ cup all-purpose flour

FOR THE FILLING

3 cups strawberries

3 teaspoons granulated sugar, divided

2 cups heavy cream

2 tablespoons powdered sugar

TO MAKE THE CAKE ROLL

1. Preheat the oven to 350°F. Line a 14-by-11-inch or similar-size baking sheet with parchment paper.

2. In a bowl using an electric mixer, beat the egg whites on medium speed until they hold stiff peaks, about 5 minutes. (Alternatively, whisk by hand for 10 to 12 minutes.) In a small bowl, beat the egg yolks, then very gently fold them into the egg whites.

3. Little by little, gently fold in the powdered sugar. Then gently fold in the flour a little at a time.

4. Pour the batter onto the prepared baking sheet and use a spatula to spread it out evenly and very thinly, about ¼ inch deep.

5. Bake for 8 to 10 minutes, until the cake is lightly golden.

6. While the cake is still warm, use the parchment paper to roll it up lengthwise. It's important to roll the cake when it is warm so it doesn't crack or break and so it cools in the proper shape. Let cool for about 20 minutes in its rolled form.

TO MAKE THE FILLING

7. Slice 1 cup of the strawberries and mix with 1 teaspoon of the granulated sugar. Set aside for the filling. Cut the remaining strawberries in half and mix with the remaining 2 teaspoons granulated sugar. Set aside for decorating the cake roll.

8. In a large bowl using a stick blender, combine the cream and powdered sugar and beat to a light and fluffy foam. Use an up-and-down motion to incorporate as much air as possible. It will take less than 1 minute. Refrigerate until ready to use.

9. To fill the cake, unroll the cake and carefully remove the parchment paper. Spread about three-quarters of the whipped cream across the cake and layer the sliced strawberries over the cream. Roll the cake back up. Spread the remaining whipped cream over the cake roll and decorate with the halved strawberries.

10. Present the cake roll on a long platter. Store on a plate covered with plastic wrap in the refrigerator for up to 2 days.

TECHNIQUE TIP

You may find it easier to flip the cake facedown onto a clean kitchen towel when you remove it from the oven and carefully remove the parchment paper while it is still hot. You can then carefully roll it up with the kitchen towel preventing the cake from sticking and giving the cake the form needed to later unroll it when it cools to fill with the whipped cream and strawberries.

 WINE PAIRING

This dessert will pair nicely with a semi dry rosé or cava like Anna de Codorníu Brut Rosé.

Churros with Hot Chocolate

CHURROS CON CHOCOLATE

Prep time: 10 minutes | Cook time: 10 minutes

Churros are so embedded in Spanish food culture that 21st century chefs are coming up with their own sophisticated twists and including them on restaurant dessert menus. You can enjoy this Spanish delight for breakfast, a morning or afternoon snack, or even at the very end of a long night. The hot chocolate is used mostly for dipping the churros. **SERVES 4**

FOR THE CHURROS

1 cup water

½ cup sugar, plus
   2½ tablespoons

½ teaspoon fine sea salt

2 tablespoons vegetable oil

1 cup all-purpose flour

Neutral oil, for deep-frying

FOR THE HOT CHOCOLATE

2¼ cups whole milk, divided

1 teaspoon cornstarch

1 cinnamon stick

½ vanilla bean, split
   lengthwise

2 cups coarsely chopped
   dark chocolate
   (63% cacao)

Pinch sea salt

Sugar

TO MAKE THE CHURROS

1. Preheat the oven to 200°F to keep the churros warm. Line a plate with paper towels.

2. In a small saucepan, combine the water, 2½ tablespoons of the sugar, the salt, and the vegetable oil. Bring to a boil over medium heat, then remove from the heat. Stir in the flour, mixing well to form a ball of dough.

3. Pour 3 inches of neutral oil into a deep skillet (no wider than 8 to 10 inches) and heat over medium-high heat to 375°F.

4. Transfer the dough to a pastry bag fitted with a medium star tip (see Tip). Pipe 5- to 6-inch lengths of the dough into the oil, using kitchen scissors to cut the dough. Fry for 2 to 4 minutes, until golden. Using a skimmer or slotted spoon, transfer the churros to the paper towel–lined plate to drain.

5. Place the remaining ½ cup sugar on a plate. Roll the churros in the sugar. Place them on a baking sheet to keep warm in the oven until the hot chocolate is ready.

6. In a small bowl, stir ¼ cup of the milk into the cornstarch and mix well so there are no lumps. Set aside.

7. In a medium saucepan, combine the remaining 2 cups milk and the cinnamon stick. Scrape the vanilla seeds into the milk and add the pod. Heat just to a boil over medium-high heat. Remove the pan from the heat, cover, and let sit for 10 minutes for the flavors to infuse.

8. Discard the vanilla pod and cinnamon stick. Add the chocolate and salt to the hot milk and stir until the chocolate melts and the mixture is well combined.

9. Restir the cornstarch mixture and add it to the chocolate mixture, whisking constantly until it dissolves. Return the pan to medium heat and stir for about 5 minutes, until it thickens. Taste and add sugar to taste, mixing it well.

10. Pour the hot chocolate into coffee cups and serve on a dessert plate with the churros alongside. Dip the churros into the thick hot chocolate to fully enjoy the treat! Store leftover churros in an airtight container at room temperature for up to 2 days. Store leftover hot chocolate in an airtight container in the refrigerator for up to 1 week.

TECHNIQUE TIP

If you don't have a pastry bag, use a freezer bag instead. Fill it with churro dough and cut a small corner of the bag. Don't cut the hole too big, though, because you want the churro thin.

Cheese Flan

FLAN DE QUESO

Prep time: 15 minutes, plus 1 hour to chill | Cook time: 35 minutes

Top this sublime dessert with sliced strawberries and raspberries coated with the remaining half of the caramel sauce. **SERVES 8**

FOR THE CARAMEL SAUCE

¾ cup sugar

3 drops fresh lemon juice

¼ cup room-
temperature water

½ cup boiling water

FOR THE FLAN

4 large eggs

¼ cup sugar

16 ounces cream cheese, at
room temperature

1. Preheat the oven to 350°F.

TO MAKE THE CARAMEL SAUCE

2. Have an 8-inch nonstick round cake pan (or similar) at the ready.

3. In a nonstick skillet, combine the sugar, lemon juice, and room-temperature water and set over medium heat. When the sugar begins to turn amber, stir it with a wooden spoon. When it turns golden and starts to bubble, remove the pan from the heat and add the boiling water while stirring. Be careful not to burn the sugar and be very careful not to burn yourself as the mixture will continue to bubble even when removed from the burner. Pour half of the caramel into a cake pan. Tilt the pan every which way to evenly coat the bottom with caramel.

TO MAKE THE FLAN

4. In a large bowl, beat the eggs. Beat in the sugar and cream cheese until light and creamy.

5. Pour the flan mixture into the pan.

6. Set the pan in a larger baking pan. Carefully pour water into the larger pan to come halfway up the sides of the cake pan.

7. Transfer the baking pan to the oven and bake for 30 minutes.

8. Remove the baking pan from the oven and carefully remove the cake pan from the water. Let the flan cool for about 15 minutes, then refrigerate for 1 hour to chill.

9. Carefully run a knife around the inside edges of the cake pan. Cover the pan with a plate and flip the flan onto the plate. Pour any caramel sauce remaining in the cake pan over the top of the flan before serving.

10. Cut it into wedges and serve on plates. Cover leftovers with plastic wrap and refrigerate for up to 5 days.

TECHNIQUE TIP

Heat the bottom of the cake pan over very low heat for 40 to 60 seconds before you unmold the flan. The caramel will melt and it will be easier to unmold.

REGIONAL VARIATION

Most regions of Spain make their flan without cheese. Some recipes call for condensed milk and include a bit of rum. These are called a Drunk Flan.

 WINE PAIRING

This dessert will pair well with a white dessert wines of the muscatel and muscat varietals.

Santiago's Torte
TARTA DE SANTIAGO

Prep time: 15 minutes | Cook time: 40 minutes

This delicious and easy cake is traditional to the Santiago pilgrimage. For an authentic presentation, cut a Cross of Saint James out of paper and place it in the middle of the cake before you dust it with powdered sugar. Brandy, Cognac, aged rum, or any sweet liqueur such as Cointreau can be substituted for the herb orujo, which is a pomace brandy infused with herbs. **SERVES 10**

1¼ cups granulated sugar

1¾ cups blanched
   almond flour

5 large eggs

Grated zest of 1 orange

Grated zest of 1 lemon

1 teaspoon ground
   cinnamon

¼ cup herb orujo or liqueur

¼ cup powdered sugar

1. Preheat the oven to 350°F. Line the bottom of an 11- or 12-inch springform pan with a round of parchment paper cut to fit.

2. In a large bowl, combine the sugar and almond flour. Add the eggs one at a time, beating vigorously until smooth after each addition. Mix in the orange and lemon zests, cinnamon, and orujo. Pour the batter into the pan.

3. Bake for about 30 minutes, or until the cake feels firm to the touch and a toothpick inserted into the center comes out clean. Remove from the oven and let cool in the pan on a wire rack for 15 minutes.

4. Remove the cake from the pan and place it on a large plate. Dust the top of the cake with the powdered sugar.

REGIONAL VARIATION

In Navarra, this cake is generally covered with apricot jam.

 WINE PAIRING

This dessert pairs well with a white dessert wine of the muscatel or muscat varietals like Ochoa from Navarra.

Spanish French Toast

TORRIJAS

Prep time: 20 minutes | Cook time: 20 minutes

This dessert is enjoyed throughout Spain year-round but especially during Holy Week. It originated in the 15th century when it was served as a tapa in bars in Madrid with wine. It is perfect to make for dessert, brunch, or an afternoon treat topped with fresh berries and homemade honey syrup (see Tip). You can use orange or lemon zest for this recipe. **SERVES 4**

---

1 lemon or orange

1 cup whole milk

1 cup heavy cream

1 cinnamon stick

1 vanilla bean, split
  lengthwise

¼ cup sugar

3 large eggs

½ cup extra-virgin olive oil
  or vegetable oil

12 slices (2 inches thick)
  day-old French bread,
  cut on the diagonal

Maple syrup, for serving

1. Using a vegetable peeler, peel off 2 wide strips of lemon zest from the lemon; be careful to not include any white pith.

2. In a medium saucepan, combine the milk, cream, cinnamon stick, and lemon zest. Scrape the vanilla seeds into the pan and add the pod. Bring just to a boil over medium-high heat. Remove from the heat and stir in the sugar until it dissolves. Cover and set aside to cool for 15 minutes.

3. In a shallow bowl, beat together the eggs.

4. Transfer the cooled milk mixture to a large bowl and remove the cinnamon stick, vanilla bean, and lemon zests.

5. Line a plate with paper towels. In a large skillet, heat the oil over medium-high heat. When hot, working in batches, dip the bread slices in the milk mixture and then into the egg.

CONTINUED

6. Place the bread in the pan and fry about 1 minute, until golden. Flip and fry the other side, about 1 minute. Place on the paper towels to drain.

7. Serve with maple syrup.

MAKE IT MORE TRADITIONAL

Serve the *torrijas* with honey syrup: In a saucepan, heat 2 tablespoons honey, 1 tablespoon brandy, and ½ cup sugar and stir until golden. Stir in ¾ cup water and heat for 10 minutes.

 WINE PAIRING

Serve torrijas for brunch with mimosas or rosé champagne. Pedro Ximénez, an intensely sweet, dark dessert sherry, will also pair nicely beautifully with it.

Sangria

Sangria is a refreshing low-alcohol aperitif usually consumed during popular summer festivities and gatherings throughout Spain. You can prepare it by mixing any type of wine with fruit, liqueur, and soda, but make sure to give the fruit time to macerate to obtain the fullest flavor and sweetness. **SERVES 4**

1 (750 ml) bottle red wine

2¼ cups orange or lemon soda

3 cups blackberries (optional)

1 cup strawberries, quartered

1 apple, diced

Grated zest and juice of 2 oranges

Grated zest and juice of 1 lemon

Grated zest and juice of 1 lime

¼ cup sugar, or to taste

1 cinnamon stick

1 vanilla bean

Dash nutmeg

3 whole cloves (optional)

½ cup rum, brandy, or Cognac

FOR SERVING

Ice

4 mint sprigs, for garnish

1. In a large pitcher, combine the wine, soda, fruit, spices, and brandy or Cognac and mix. Let the fruit macerate for 2 to 3 hours, or even overnight in the refrigerator.

2. To serve, fill large wineglasses with ice and pour the sangria over it. Garnish each glass with a sprig of fresh mint.

DIFFERENT SPIN

Rosé or white sangrias are also very refreshing during the summertime. For white sangria, use wine that has not been aged in oak and gin or vodka in place of the rum or brandy.

Lemon Summer Shandy

CLARA DE LIMÓN

Prep time: 5 minutes

A lemon shandy is sangria's little sister and is as popular and refreshing—but a lot quicker and easier to prepare. All you need is your favorite type of beer, lemon soda or lemonade, and plenty of ice. Those with a sweet tooth should go with a sweeter soda or lemonade. **MAKES 1 SHANDY**

Ice	1 part lemon soda or	Grated lemon zest
1 part beer	lemonade	

Fill a large wineglass or beer goblet to the top with ice. Pour in the beer followed by the soda. Stir. Top it off with lemon zest and enjoy!

DIFFERENT SPIN

For a less-sweet version, make it with lemon-scented sparkling water or lemon Italian soda.

Gin and Tonic

Prep time: 5 minutes

Spaniards take great pride in their reimagining of the British G&T, and gin and tonic mixology has been taken to a higher level, becoming a social ritual among Spanish gin lovers. They have accented the complex flavors and aromas of the gin and the tonic with a host of complementary garnishes and serve the drink impeccably over ice in a large fish bowl-style wineglass. So do as the Spaniards do and offer your guests a G&T after dinner with a bowl of gummy bears! **MAKES 1 COCKTAIL**

Ice
2 parts gin
3 parts tonic

GARNISH OPTIONS
Citrus fruit: lemon twist, lime twist, grapefruit twist, orange twist
Spices: coriander, cardamom, juniper berries, black peppercorns, pink peppercorns, star anise

Fresh herbs: mint, cilantro, basil, rosemary, thyme, parsley
Roots: grated fresh ginger
Other: cucumber, rose petals, edible flowers

1. Decide upon and prepare the garnishes that you will use.

2. Fill a large, open wineglass with ice.

3. Pour the gin over the ice followed by the tonic water. Stir with a cocktail spoon, add your preferred garnishes, and enjoy!

G&T TIPS

Decide which type of gin you prefer: botanical and herbaceous or dry. Use premium tonic water. It will make a difference. Never garnish it with a lemon or lime wedge. Always use a large twist of citrus zest with no white pith on it. Although there are many charts that tell you what garnish pairs best with what gin, it is really a matter of taste. I love my G&T with a dry gin, such as Martin Miller, garnished with juniper berries, cardamom, pink peppercorns, edible flowers, and a nice size lemon twist. Always pour it in a large and open glass similar to a wineglass.

G&T SERVING

A fun idea for a gathering is to set up a G&T bar with small vases full of fresh herbs, test tubes with an array of spices, and a small plate with the prepared citrus twists. Include a variety of types of gin and tonic waters.

Measurement Conversions

	U.S. Standard	U.S. Standard (ounces)	Metric (approximate)
VOLUME EQUIVALENTS (LIQUID)	2 tablespoons	1 fl. oz.	30 mL
	¼ cup	2 fl. oz.	60 mL
	½ cup	4 fl. oz.	120 mL
	1 cup	8 fl. oz.	240 mL
	1½ cups	12 fl. oz.	355 mL
	2 cups or 1 pint	16 fl. oz.	475 mL
	4 cups or 1 quart	32 fl. oz.	1 L
	1 gallon	128 fl. oz.	4 L
VOLUME EQUIVALENTS (DRY)	⅛ teaspoon	———	0.5 mL
	¼ teaspoon	———	1 mL
	½ teaspoon	———	2 mL
	¾ teaspoon	———	4 mL
	1 teaspoon	———	5 mL
	1 tablespoon	———	15 mL
	¼ cup	———	59 mL
	⅓ cup	———	79 mL
	½ cup	———	118 mL
	⅔ cup	———	156 mL
	¾ cup	———	177 mL
	1 cup	———	235 mL
	2 cups or 1 pint	———	475 mL
	3 cups	———	700 mL
	4 cups or 1 quart	———	1 L
	½ gallon	———	2 L
	1 gallon	———	4 L
WEIGHT EQUIVALENTS	½ ounce	———	15 g
	1 ounce	———	30 g
	2 ounces	———	60 g
	4 ounces	———	115 g
	8 ounces	———	225 g
	12 ounces	———	340 g
	16 ounces or 1 pound	———	455 g

	Fahrenheit (F)	Celsius (C) (approximate)
OVEN TEMPERATURES	250°F	120°C
	300°F	150°C
	325°F	180°C
	375°F	190°C
	400°F	200°C
	425°F	220°C
	450°F	230°C

Ingredient and Equipment Resources

Ingredients

Bomba rice: La Tienda (Tienda.com) and Gourmet Food Store (GourmetFoodStore.com)

Pimentón de la Vera: Hot and sweet smoked paprika. La Tienda (Tienda.com)

Piparras peppers: Semisweet Basque peppers. La Tienda (Tienda.com)

Spanish albacore tuna: Bonito del norte. La Tienda (Tienda.com) and iGourmet.com

Spanish anchovy fillets: Nardin Anchovy Fillets or Anxoves de l'Escala. La Tienda (Tienda.com)

Spanish chorizo: Palacios Extra Quality Sweet or Extra Quality Spicy Chorizo (Palacios-en.com/p/products/chorizo)

Spanish saffron: Spice Jungle (SpiceJungle.com) and La Tienda (Tienda.com)

Spanish squid ink: El Sison Squid Ink/4 Pack. Gourmet Food Store (GourmetFoodStore.com) and Artisanal Foods (ArtisanalFoods.com)

Equipment

Frittata/tortilla pan (hinged): La Tienda (Tienda.com), Macy's (Macys.com), and Wayfair (Wayfair.com)

Large mortar: Wayfair (Wayfiar.com) and Crate and Barrel (CrateandBarrel.com)

Paella pan: La Tienda (Tienda.com) and Williams Sonoma (Williams-Sonoma.com)

Terra cotta cazuela: La Tienda (Tienda.com)

Index

Acknowledgments

To my husband, Luis, with whom I have eaten my way throughout Spain. We have enjoyed the best food, from the quaintest little restaurants in tiny villages to the Michelin-starred. Our love for food is our secret ingredient, which has bound us together forever.

To our dear friend Mariano, Uncle Mari to our kids, who has been our inseparable gastronomic companion and with whom we have explored every corner in every region of Spain. I hope this book inspires you to write the "Marianin Guide."

To my beloved and eternal supporters Regi, Edu, and Adri, who I am proud to say have inherited our passion for food and at a very young age could distinguish between olive oil made with Arbequina and Picudo olives! You are a clear and gratifying example of our effort to expose and educate you on world food cultures.

To my in-laws Cristina and Ramon, thank you for your unconditional, constant support throughout the years, and Ramon . . . for being my Spanish cuisine mentor.

To Rachid, my dear friend and business partner at Norema Salinas catering in Madrid! For taking the reins of the business, winning our clientele, and making it possible for me to be here with my family. The inspiration of your delicious and elegantly balanced cuisine has been invaluable.

To my dear friend Lori Tenny, the reason this book came to life. For your support, trust, and belief in me. I could not have done this without you.

To my dearest friend Sol and her mom, Maru, thank you for your invaluable pastry-making tips and all of the absolutely delicious "rosquillas" you have made for me throughout the years!

About the Author

Norema Salinas is an international food maven specializing in Spanish food, culture, and entertainment. She has lived in Madrid for a great portion of her life and traveled extensively throughout Spain with her husband and three children, who are Spanish. She was a pioneer of modern Spanish catering in Spain in the 1990s with her company Norema Salinas Catering, which she now codirects with her business partner while she lives in the San Francisco Bay Area. She has been back in California since the summer of 2015, when she and her business partner brought Scirocco Wind pop-ups (Spanish-Moroccan cuisine theme) to the Bay Area for a few months. She is presently working in catering and event production for Betty Zlatchin Catering in San Francisco, where she is successfully implementing her expertise and international food knowledge.

CPSIA information can be obtained
at www.ICGtesting.com
Printed in the USA
JSHW080719020123
35616JS00005B/58